ST🖕P SELLING MUSIC

Career-Changing Lessons For Musicians

DAMIAN KEYES

DK PUBLISHING
30 Brunswick Street East, Hove, BN3 1AU

First published in 2019 by DK Publishing

STOP SELLING MUSIC
Copyright © 2019 by Damian Keyes

ISBN 978-1-9996153-2-1

Front cover design: Tom Heron
Interior design and layout: Henry Hyde

This book is dedicated to Ella. Thank you for all the adventures, the support and the love you show me every day. You make me want to be the best me I can be and show you every day how happy you make me. You are my one more minute!

CONTENTS

Introduction 11

Part One: Practising 16

Recording yourself
Seeking out self-improvement
Obsession helps
To click or not to click ... there is no question
What to practise
You've got the power
Where and when to practise
Practise makes perfect
Play stuff that you love
The art of simplicity

Part Two: Song Writing 26

Top line melodies
Auto-tune
Lyrics and subject matter
Stealing
Arrangements
Song writing lessons

Part Three: Rehearsing 30

Planning your rehearsal
Breaking songs down to make them tight
Rehearsing the show not the songs
The marketing opportunity
Record and document your rehearsal
The etiquette of rehearsals
Set List construction

Part Four: Performing 39

Who are you?
Gig etiquette
How to front a band
Stage presence
What to wear on stage

The pace of the gig
When it all goes wrong

Part Five: Touring 48
Eating and staying healthy
How not to kill your band mates
How to maximise time on the road
Don't just create memories, document them
Friday drive day
Dealing with sound limiters
The gods of the gigs – the music industry's dark secret
Hygiene
No pooping on the tour bus
Relationship sacrifices

Part Six: Gear 58
Gear does not maketh a god
The festival set up
Take pride in your gear
The stories behind your gear
Spare gear
Using other bands' gear

Part Seven: Marketing 65
Photos
Videos
Networking
How you're contactable
Merchandise
The power of sold out
Social media
Show off every aspect of what you do

Part Eight: Money 74
You wouldn't expect a plumber
The power of free
Knowing your worth
Investing in yourself
How many gigs should you be doing a year?

See your day job as an investor in your dream
Sacrifice for the long-term
Teaching vs covers as supplementary income
Stop selling music

Part Nine: Life Lessons   85

The importance of driving
Taking the rough with the smooth
Becoming unstoppable or irreplaceable
Finding the positives
The art of control
Don't be a dick
It's going to be OK
Taking constructive criticism
Dealing with haters

Part Ten: Self-Management   97

What do you want?
Motorway analogy
The art of focus
Time-management vs priority management
Time-keeping tips
Learning songs

Conclusion   103

30 Day Challenge   105

A last favour   123

Acknowledgements   124

Introduction

Back in the day, which was a Wednesday, music used to be attached to a physical product – such as a record, cassette tape or CD – and selling this physical product was where musicians would make most of their money. And it was possible to make a lot of money due to the sizeable profit margin between the price it cost to produce an album in record, cassette or CD form and the price at which it retailed. For example, a CD would cost about £2 to make but could retail for as much as £20. Musicians would release singles as a loss leader and go on tour in order to promote sales of their album. Back then the profit margin on gig tickets was pretty low as it was all about funnelling people towards buying the album. But then, in 1999, Napster came along and allowed people to illegally download music and from there the floodgates opened. Along came the likes of Spotify and Apple, providing music in digital form instead of something physical you could actually hold.

Everything changed in that moment. And so in today's society, the general public's idea of buying music is spending ten pounds or dollars per month on a streaming service like Spotify. And they don't even have to spend that if they're prepared to put up with adverts. Instantly, you can see how much less money is being spent on music. People used to spend more than ten pounds or dollars on one album. Now they're effectively paying it for the 50 million or so tracks on Spotify, and this usually converts to about 1p per five or six listens for the artist. So, if you have one million listens on Spotify, you'll make around £5,000. Imagine if you sold one million copies of an album back in the day – it would have made £15-20 million in revenue. OK, so the artist wouldn't have received all of that but it goes to show that the amount of money being made from music today is very different.

The bad news is, these days an album doesn't make any money. But the good news is, you can still make money as a musician, you just need to attach your music to something else that's sellable. This can be a really hard concept to get your head around at first, as we're so conditioned to assume that we should be selling our music. But the hard truth is, people are no longer buying music. CD sales have fallen 90% in last 16 years. The year 2000 was the biggest ever selling year for the CD – 943 million were sold in the US alone. But in 2018 that figure had dropped to 52 million.

You could argue that vinyl sales have gone up recently but that's mainly down to what I call the 'avocado effect'. If you'd bought vinyl ten years ago you'd have been considered a creepy motherfucker but right now it's cool because the type of hipsters who eat smashed avo out of a flowerpot have deemed

11

it so. Vinyl might be trendy right now but if you think it's going to save the music industry you are wrong. For a start, so many of the records sold today are reissues of old albums and not from new bands. And records are a lot harder to play than streaming. Listening to vinyl is way more of an experience thing, and yes, the sound quality of vinyl might be better, but sadly the only people who really care about that are sound geeks.

Another argument I often come up against is from musicians who sell CDs at their gigs. 'We're still able to sell our music,' they tell me. But is it really their music they're selling? Most people who buy CDs at a gig do so in order to have a memento of a great night. Chances are they'll never actually play it. They'll view the CD as a piece of merch and stream the band's music when they want to hear it. Effectively they're buying a souvenir from the night, they're not buying music. And anyway, selling a handful of CDs at a show is not enough to earn a living from. You also have to produce CDs in bulk, with the risk that you could end up with a thousand of them stuffed under your bed.

At the moment, a lot of musicians are caught in a weird kind of limbo, still trying to sell music even though people have stopped buying it. When they promote a new album or EP they give their audience a mixed message, asking them to buy it on the one hand but also telling them it's available via the usual streaming services. The trouble with this approach is that it confuses the message and ultimately, if you give a person two options and one of them is to pay and the other is free, it's not hard to guess which one most people will choose.

So that's why this book is called *Stop Selling Music*. I want you to have a powerful and profitable strategy and to be promoting a clear message when it comes to your music, which is: *'Our music's out now, listen to it for free here...'* When I made a video with the same title as this book I received a LOT of hate and I do appreciate that this message can be hard to hear. I absolutely believe that musicians should be rewarded for their work and I 100% believe that music should be paid for. Music changes lives; it provides the soundtrack to our lives, but we have to face reality. PEOPLE ARE NO LONGER BUYING MUSIC. Think about it, how many record stores are there in your town now? How many people do you know who still have a home stereo system as the focal point of their living room? You need to start seeing your music as something you give away for free – and here's the important part – *in order to monetise elsewhere.*

I receive a lot of messages from musicians who understand what I'm saying but are still reluctant to let go of the dream of selling an album or EP. To them I say, it's time to be all in, don't let your ego or fear stop you. All that matters now is finding a new way to monetise your talent and your art and that's what this book is about. I still believe that your music should be attached to something, and in this book I'm going to go into a lot of detail about the different ways in which you can do this, but in a nutshell it's about attaching your music to other things in order to build a following of super fans. Once you have a tribe of people who are invested in you you'll be able to sell to them.

Try releasing a new song for free every few weeks on your social media and make a music video, performance video and story video for them, so you've attached the music to something tangible. See YouTube videos as the new CDs. By giving people something to watch as well as listen to, you're giving people more reasons to become invested in you.

Provide your audience with regular updates and stories about your band and your performances, in order to build investment in your brand, then hit them with a request to buy something. When I'm explaining this concept to bands I liken it to a computer game like *Street Fighter or Mortal Combat.* In order to do the special move you have to build up the special move bar by taking part in the game. Once you've done enough fighting your energy bar becomes full and you can make your move. If you try to do it too soon you'll fail. As a musician you need to build up an investment from people before you ask them to do something. And every time you ask them to do something or buy something you wipe that bar clean and it will need building back up again. The good thing is, the more value you put into your content and socials and looking after people, the more that bar builds. And you'd be surprised what people will do if that bar is on 100%.

The trouble is, a lot of musicians only want to put about 1% into the bar before using it. But this is like the dude who sends a dick pic straight away. Most girls will instantly delete. They're counting on catching that one person who happens to be in the right mood – or with the right kind of daddy issues – in order to get lucky. Treating your music career like this is like playing a lottery. People who can't be arsed to put the effort in won't succeed. And it's so important that you're putting the effort into the right areas.

A band came through to me this morning saying they'd sold 70 copies of their CD, which is amazing given that people can get that same music for free. But what if they'd put that work into building their audience by providing free music and added value, then monetised that larger audience? They could have ended up selling hundreds more of that product, whether it be a t-shirt or a book of pictures from their tour, and they probably would have made a lot more money.

I understand how hard it can be to let go of the old way of doing things – in many ways what I'm saying is like challenging an old and established religion. But ultimately, it's still about the music and being the best musician you can be, it's just the monetising part that's changed. This book is about not leaving things to chance and hoping you'll get your lucky break. It's about kicking the door down and showing the world what you've got. It's about ensuring you're the best musician you can be, with the best strategy, playing the most amount of gigs in front of the most amount of people and taking control of every opportunity. I hope this book helps you to analyse what you're doing and reset the bar to where it needs to be. In a lot of bands there tends to be one person who does all the organising. If you are that person I want this book to help you recognise how to make your life easier and fix this.

This book can be read through from start to finish, but you can also use it as a manual, dipping into the sections that are most applicable to you at any given time. In the section on **Practising** we look at how taking your playing seriously will help you stand out in a noisy world and how success is so often down to what you practise rather than how much. The **Song Writing** section will get you thinking and acting like a professional songwriter and help you to focus on writing for other people. In the section on **Rehearsing** we focus on the structure of your rehearsals. The days of bringing a load of tinnies and messing about with your mates are gone – if you want to blow people away on stage you have to take rehearsals seriously. The **Performing** section is a huge one for me because musicians have the opportunity to do so much at a gig and yet so often they don't take advantage of this. In this section we'll look at the art of marketing yourself at a gig – whether it's in a pub or a stadium – and how successful pub gigging can ultimately lead to a stadium tour. In **Touring** I want to help you deal with the gruelling aspects of life on the road and show you how to stay healthy and happy – and not kill any of your bandmates! I also want to help you get clear on whether life on the road is for you – it definitely isn't for everyone. In the section on **Gear** we'll look at how gear does not make a god and is not nearly as important as so many people make out. I'll show you how you can save a lot of valuable time, money and energy by setting yourself up with basic, industry standard gear. There's nothing wrong with collecting gear but if the money you're spending could be spent on other things like Facebook ads then it's going to get in the way of you achieving success. It's time to stop guitar collecting and start career building! In **Marketing** we're going to take a close look at things like your image, photos, videos and website and I'll help you build a strong personal brand and simplify your social media. At the moment musicians are making social media a lot more complicated than it needs to be. In this section I'll help you prioritise what you need to be doing on your socials and avoid the trap of being all things to all people and the stress that entails. In **Money** I want to smash the myths about how hard it is to achieve financial success in the music industry. I want to show you how, with the right attitude, making money can be relatively easy. The **Life Lessons** section includes all the magical real-life stuff that I wish someone had told me back when I was starting out, rather than having to learn it all the hard way. And in the final section, on **Self Management**, we'll look at how you can start putting everything from this book into practise and implement all you've learned.

Over the years, I've taught thousands of musicians and hired of hundreds of musicians (and auditioned thousands in order to hire those hundreds) and the one thing that's become obvious to me is that, while there are millions of musicians out there all wanting the same thing, I truly believe that success is there for the taking. It all comes down to being prepared to work hard enough and at the right things. Then the privilege of having a music career is 100% attainable. So let's get started!

Part One: Practising

Before we begin, I want you to get really honest with yourself and ask yourself this question: *Are you good enough?* THE best way to ensure a long term, successful career is to simply be better than everyone else. Your first job is to be able to compete with the musicians getting the work that you want. The good news is that you have control over this. The hours and hours of practice you put in during those years when you first fell in love with being a musician is likely to already be making a difference. Think of your practice as similar to putting money into the bank; every hour you play is a deposit, building your investment.

When I look back to how I was when I started playing (and for many years after) the word I would use to describe my behaviour would be 'obsessive'. The hours and hours and hours I spent improving my playing meant that when my professional journey as a musician began, I was capable and ready. Practice takes discipline and it's about what and how you practice and not just what you fancy playing at that moment. It's about pushing yourself, or finding someone who will push you, to become the best that you can be.

Recording yourself

How can you tell if you're improving in your music unless you have something to compare it to? The best way to compare your old playing with your new is by recording yourself when you practise. When I was starting out I used to record myself on an old four-track recorder. Who remembers the days of pressing record and play together to record onto a cassette?! It was a hassle but I did it so that I could listen to what was actually coming out of my fingers rather than what was going on in my head. Hearing a recording of yourself playing for the first time can be a bit like listening to your voice on an answerphone message – *is that really how I speak*?? But it's worth any initial discomfort because it makes it so much easier to identify what needs working on. And the best thing about recording yourself practising today is that you can do it for free on your phone – and you can do it in video as well as audio, so you can even watch your technique. I need to tell you now, I'm a technique Nazi. I can pretty much spot a good bass player from the moment they take their guitar out and place it on their lap. For the fifteen years I was working at ACM and BIMM one of my jobs would be to assess every student who wanted to study bass at the college. I would listen to them play for 15 minutes in order to judge which course they should be on. In the vast majority of cases I'd be able to predict from the way they held their instrument whether they should be on the degree, GCSE or A level course. If the bass was too high or too low, or where they placed their right hand thumb told me if they were going to be a powerful or weak bass player.

Take some time to study the technique of an expert in your musical field. Then record yourself practising and compare the two. Your job isn't to mimic your musical heroes but to learn from them. Musical talent might be subjective but authority isn't, it's either there or it's not. Playing in tune, playing in time and authority can all be improved by recording yourself practicing. Record yourself from different angles so you can see as much of yourself as possible. Genius is in the attention to detail. If you're videoing yourself from the front you might not be able to tell if you're hunched over. How you stand really affects how you play or sing and the power of your performance. So, when you watch yourself back, ask *how am I standing/sitting? Am I relaxed? Are my hands and body in the right position?* When you record yourself on a regular basis you'll be able to pick up on these nuances. It's also a great way to see how you are improving, which can be hugely motivating.

Seeking out self-improvement

Musicians tend to be really proud of being self-taught but I believe that everyone should have some kind of mentor. The fact is, all of us are taught to some extent, even if it's just from studying our favourite musicians on records or YouTube videos, we'll be picking up details from other players. Finding someone to bounce ideas off is massively helpful, especially to make sure you're not picking up bad habits, which is all too easy to do if self-taught. The fact is, if you want to be professional at anything, why would you not want a teacher? I'm a professional business person with a couple of million pound companies but I'm still looking for guidance when it comes to my business. If Roger Federer played his tennis coach he'd win every game but without that coach he wouldn't be the best in the world. The coach is there to take an overview of his game and help him get better. Similarly, a mentor will give you an overview of your music and technique and show you how to improve and what you need to learn. A lot of musicians leave music college and assume that they're done with learning but I think this is a seriously limiting belief and could be massively detrimental to your career. If you don't keep learning and challenging yourself to try new things you'll just be regurgitating the same thing every time you tour and it becomes like paint by numbers. You need someone to keep pushing you to improve and enjoy playing – you need the excitement factor.

Finding a playing mentor or coach will make you more employable and enthusiastic and give you the confidence to take on the kind of gigs you've never have done before. Look for experienced teachers as opposed to experienced musicians, although they can be both. The key thing is that they're good at communicating, and it's well worth seeking out the best. Even if you only have a handful of lessons at £100 per hour rather than £30 and have to travel three hours to get there, a good mentor will give you valuable ideas to work on for the next few months. Mentorship is different to music lessons, it's more a case of having a coaching session as and when you need it rather than a weekly lesson.

Bruce Dickinson was my music mentor for years – and has been my overall career mentor – but I've had several bass mentors too; people who've made me try things I haven't done before, who've pushed me to grow and improve. The best way to find a good mentor is via word of mouth, or look online for tutors, be it in your local area or someone prepared to Skype with you, then ask to have a meeting. At that initial meeting tell them that you're looking for a mentor and where you'd like to get to with your playing, or even songwriting. Approach them with a goal in mind as it helps them know what they'd be helping you work towards and if it fits their specialism. If they say no don't be put off just find someone else.

Obsession helps

True story – I'm a very obsessive person. This also means that I'm a very limited person in a lot of ways because it's impossible to obsess about a lot of things at once. Before I got into business I only had one passion, bass playing. Between the ages of 15 and 23 everything was about the bass to me. When I got dressed in the morning I'd put on my trousers, t-shirt and bass and wear it like it was a piece of clothing. I'd walk around the house playing until I wanted something to eat, and even then I probably wouldn't take it off. As far as I was concerned everything else in life interrupted my bass playing, it was never the other way round. I believe that having a career as a musician and being paid to do what you love is a privilege not a right and that privilege needs to be earned through being good enough. There's only one way to be good enough and that's through the very time-consuming process of learning, experimenting, practising and experience. If you want it badly enough you have to become slightly obsessed. You have to make the time to get better, you have to prioritise your music over watching Netflix or going out with friends.

Of course, this isn't easy. When I was first starting out as a musician my girlfriend and I never had much money to spend on holidays so we'd tend to go camping. I'd always pack my guitar and as we didn't have much space in our little car I'd pack it in a soft case, a truly heroic compromise, I know. But obviously I'd never leave my guitar in the car at night because I didn't want it to get nicked, or cold. So I'd bring extra blankets to wrap it in and bring it in the tent with me. I mean with us, with my girlfriend and me. Don't worry, I didn't actually spoon the guitar, well, only occasionally. I'm so sorry if you're reading this Tash. My guitar was always the other woman in our relationship.

People don't like it when I say you need to be obsessed in order to succeed, probably for reasons like the one detailed above! But it's more a case of matching your obsession levels with how much you want to achieve. Often, when people tell me I'm wrong about the need to be obsessed, it's because they want to justify their own lack of work. But if you want the privilege of a life as a professional musician then you have to put the work in. It's a sliding scale. If you want to make an average living as a bass player it just needs an average amount of work, but if you want to tour the world and be the best then it requires obsession. You need to match your work ethic to your dreams. I can't stress enough that it's fine if you don't want to be world class, you just need to get clear on your goals and match your work ethic accordingly. If you want to play just for the fun of it you've already won. But if you want to tour the world your guitar has to become like an extra limb. The fact is, the more effort you put into something, the better you will become.

To click or not to click... there is no question

There seems to be a debate amongst musicians over whether you should use a click when practicing, or whether it 'takes away from the feel man!' First of all, a click is not a condom! A click is a way to naturally stay in time. I highly recommend practising to a metronome because it won't vary on its timing and that's what will make you tight as a musician.

> *The more time you spend practising to a metronome,*
> *the more you're going to become a natural at playing in time.*

It shocks me how many musicians not only don't practice with a click but even argue that they shouldn't because the feel is lost if the playing is too rigid. This is nonsense because, unlike 'the feel', playing in time isn't subjective. If a band isn't locking in together they don't sound tight and they won't be good live. Manipulating your timing is a very powerful thing. Once you can play bang on with a click then you can move your note placement. If you're playing behind the beat you get a much more powerful, authoritative sound. If you play just in front of the beat you get a very exciting, slightly out of control feel.

As a musician you can manipulate the timing to control the feel but you have to learn to control your timing first in order to be able to do so. If you're not practising with a click you won't be able to speed up or slow down accordingly. The drummers Brad Wilk from Rage Against the Machine and Chad Smith from the Chilli Peppers both have the ability to play with huge power. They're both very heavy hitters but they pull the feel of the track back by playing behind the beat, creating a very lazy, powerful feel. But if you listen to the first Arctic Monkeys album, the drummer is pushing the click slightly in front of the beat, creating an exciting, frantic, almost nervous feel. But in each of these examples the drummers had to learn how to do it right before they could do it 'wrong'.

It's never been easier to get a metronome as you can download one from the app store for free. In terms of practising it's harder to play something slower than faster. For those who think playing to a click is easy and want a challenge, play a shuffle groove at forty beats per minute. Also look at subdivisions of notes, it doesn't have to stay in 4/4. Why not try some more complex time signatures like 5/4 or 9/8? Pay attention to the dynamic of the feel of the notes against the timing. For example, if you play a shuffle groove at forty beats per minute, you can experiment with the emphasis on the notes.

Playing with a metronome is like playing along to the world's best drummer. If you still think a click takes away the feel go and listen to Rosanna by Toto and tell me there's no feel in that hi-hat part. You also need to keep practising with a metronome or your timing will go off. With age and experience you gain authority in your playing but your timing and technique can still get a little bit wobbly. It's exactly the same with sports. If you're an athlete and you don't keep up with your training your performance will suffer. When I was playing there was never a time when I didn't practise with a click. It was a no-brainer to me, why wouldn't I practise with something that would keep me in time?

What to practise

What to practise is more important than how much you practise, especially as over-practice can lead to repetitive strain injury. The problem is that musicians tend to practise what they like rather than what they need to improve upon. So the first thing you need to do is get clear on how you can achieve the most from your practice. It could be that you want to improve your sight reading, or you need to improve your technique, your sound or even your range as a singer. All of these will require different types of practice, focused on the area needing improvement and not trying to do everything at once. For example, if vibrato is something personal to you, how much time do you spend on your vibrato (if you play a melodic instrument)? How many musicians sit playing the same note for hours a day just to practise that one detail? Or studying other musicians to see how every player's vibrato differs? That's why rehearsal rooms are full of guitarists and singers with shrill, out of tune vibratos. The same goes for bass players' right hand technique or a drummer's snare consistency. It's about analysing and looking at how it can be improved.

Practice is all about breaking down your playing and building it up again. This is what you need to do, whatever you want to achieve. Breaking things down, both in terms of tempo and technique, helps you avoid practising your mistakes. For example, if you're trying to play a three octave G major scale and you're playing it a bit too fast for your ability, you'll keep messing up and by doing so, you'll also be programming your brain to put the mistakes in.

Start slowly and patiently analyse what you're doing. If you use a metronome and slow it down by 20 or 30 beats per minute you can focus on practising something perfectly at that speed. Once you've got it right you can slowly start to increase the speed, a bit like building up a muscle. It's all about learning with the right foundations.

> *Your job is not to practise something until you get it right,*
> *but to practise it until you can't play it wrong.*

It's so important to be patient and meticulous. I know this can be frustrating, but the more you practise in the short term, the more it will pay off in the long term. And whatever you're practising will help your playing across the board because you're training the dexterity and motor memory of your fingers. So, even though it's frustrating and time consuming, remember that you're not just practising a riff, you're practising the entirety of your technique.

Improvisation is very different from practising technique – it's a bit like art compared to maths. So much of art comes from improvisation and experimentation, but you need to nail the technique first before you can start to look at what you're trying to say through your music. It's very difficult to truly improvise and not just play licks you've already played a million times before. Rhythms are more important than the note choice in a melody. Try this exercise now: pick up your instrument (or drum on the table or sing to yourself) and improvise with either one or two notes max. Try and play or sing a solo with a maximum of two notes, or an emotional piece of music using just one singular note and only using different rhythms. Trying to improvise a 12 bar solo using two notes and a multitude of rhythms takes the emphasis away from patterns. Doing this means you have to be creative with note length and rhythms but you can't be creative with the notes themselves. The benefit of this exercise is that it will make you think more about the rhythms and the spaces as a way of creating emotion, rather than just a flurry of notes. If you can improve using just two notes, you can definitely improve with all of them.

My final piece of advice on what to practise is the importance of being very clear on what you want to achieve from each session. Instead of having five or six goals, I'd have one, e.g. sight reading practice, or technique practice.

You've got the power

Something I find hugely ironic is that musicians will spend thousands on gear without paying any real attention to their hands, fingers, diaphragm or feet. The fact is, *you* are the sound of your instrument. Flea from the Chilli Peppers will sound like Flea, whether he's playing on a £500 bass or a £10,000 bass because he has all of his Flea-isms in his hands. Even though a lot of us play electric instruments, they have acoustic properties, which means if you hit something gently and then hit it hard it's not just the volume that changes, it's the frequency. It's the same if you pat your leg gently and then pat it hard. You're not just changing the volume, you're changing the sound. It's your job to figure out how to get the right frequency from your instrument. That why the power will always come from a musician's body first and foremost rather than any piece of equipment they're using. It's a bit like the world-class Brazilian footballers who learned their skills playing barefoot as kids. When you get to world class level as a footballer having expensive boots might make that extra five percent of difference but they weren't what was needed to get them to that level in the first place – it was their feet pure and simple.

> *A musician's first priority should be figuring out how to use their body to make their instrument sound good.*

If you hit your instrument (with acoustic properties) too hard you choke the note and it will sound very harsh. Of course this is all subjective, you might deliberately want to distort the note. Listen to Gary Moore tear into a guitar solo vs how delicate John Mayer's playing can be. There's a noticeable difference in their note definition because this is how they've chosen to play. But, just as with manipulating your timing, you have to get really good at the basics first in order to get to choose. It's exactly the same for singers. You get to choose whether you want to put grit and power into your voice or whether you want it to be velvety smooth, for example Kelly Jones from the Stereophonics versus Michael Bublé.

Practise playing around with the dynamics to find out where you want to sit on the spectrum. And practise different styles so you're able to emulate as many as possible. This isn't about copying other people but being able to choose from all the different flavours and ingredients available to put into your playing. Respect other people's sounds and styles. You might not like their sound but understanding how they developed it is important. You don't have to implement it into your own playing but the more you respect and understand other people's techniques, the more control it gives you as a player and the less one dimensional you become.

Where and when to practise

The biggest excuse musicians use for not practising is lack of time. It was something I heard over and over again when I was teaching bass. The fact is, if you're not allocating enough time to your practice, it's more of a priority issue. There are so many places you can practise and you don't even need to have your instrument in your hand. You can practise singing and drumming and dexterity exercises in the shower or on the loo or in the car. I can practise bass playing in my head. I can sit in a car and listen to a piece of music and study the notes they're hitting.

Come up with creative ways to be able to practise. For example, you could use ad breaks on TV for three or four minutes of practice, or how about on your lunch break at work? That's a solid hour a day! Even your commute home can be a creative opportunity to practice. It's a bit like high intensity training. You might not have the time to do a marathon but you can do a sprint. And sprinting in regular short bursts definitely improves your performance.

I saw a great example of a musician being creative with when and where to practise when I was on a gig once. We got to the venue, unloaded our gear from the van, set up, did the sound-check and then went to the pub to wait. We played our first set for an hour, then had a half hour break before our final set. During the break we all went to the bar to chill, apart from the drummer. He was nowhere to be seen. It turned out he'd gone to the van to practise on a practise pad. He was so committed to improving as a musician he even practised in a break mid gig! This guy is now one of the world's most respected drummers and he reached that level because he puts the work in whenever and wherever he can. Five minutes here, five minutes there, it all adds up.

Practice makes perfect

People are always looking for shortcuts when it comes to improving but there isn't a magic formula – it really is a case of knowing what to practise and then slogging it out. The fastest way to improve is by putting the hours in and improving is vital if you want the privilege of life as a professional musician. You have to be able to compete with the other people out there already doing what you want to do and the best way you can do this is by being better than them. Make sure you're practising in all of the areas you want and need to get better in. If you put time into playing in your bedroom you'll get better at technique. As a bass player, I've done close to 2,000 gigs, so I'm very good at playing bass in that live environment, at maintaining the energy and the groove, at covering for myself and others should something go wrong, and at creating a buzz. But I'm nowhere near as experienced at recording in a studio. I'd definitely be more exposed in a studio environment because I've probably only been in a studio about fifty times, so I'm much less practised there. If you have a specific end goal you can make your practise more targeted. For example, if you want to be a studio musician, then practise recording yourself at every opportunity. You can do it for free every day on your phone. The more time you put in the better you get. Simple.

Play stuff that you love

When I was about 17 and I was going through my full on obsession with bass playing I used to practise to jazz CDs. This was because I aspired to be the best I could be and everyone said jazz was the most technical expression. I'd listen to amazing musicians but after about the second track all I wanted to do was put on some Metallica. I really wanted to like jazz, but I wasn't inspired by it because it wasn't what I wanted to play, but I could sit and learn from musicians I love all day. It's really important to expand your musical knowledge but not at the expense of enjoying what you do. If I was going to have a bass in my hand for six hours a day, I needed to enjoy it. The most fun times I've had as a musician have been when I've been playing for *me*. Seek out the musicians who inspire you and watch, learn from and play along with them. Find YouTube tutorials based around your favourite individual players. You have to do whatever it takes to keep your passion alive and keep that fire burning.

The art of simplicity

I think there's a real lesson to be had in the ability to play simple things to a very high standard. It's so easy to overlook the power of simplicity. The bass in *With or Without You* by U2 is basically the same four notes played again and again. But whenever I hear other people play it they never sound as good as Adam Clayton. I think this is down to a lack of respect – people don't take it seriously because they think it's easy. But to play something 'easy' at a world class level is difficult. You need to respect the sound, the power, the groove, the technique that goes into it. People think that, because it's only four notes, anyone can play it. But there's a reason why Clayton's the guy playing it in stadiums every night. The power it requires to hold things down so that The Edge can layer things over the rhythm section and put the emotion into the song is off the scale. The discipline needed to be able to do that bar after bar, song after song, night after night is immense.

Many years ago, at BIMM, we did a masterclass with a drummer called John 'JR' Robinson, who's the most recorded drummer in history. He's also played with Michael Jackson and recorded the drums on the *Off The Wall* album. One of the tracks he played for us was *Billie Jean*, which he played live with MJ. It's the most meat and potatoes groove you'll hear – bass, snare, bass, snare. Robinson called it 'the money groove', in other words it was what he got paid to do. Every detail of that groove was perfect, from the control to the consistency of the snare and the timing, he didn't wobble one bit. It was the simplest thing to play but I've never heard anyone play it like that, it was jaw-dropping. To reach that level of perfection takes years of practice. And if you look at most paid gigs, it's usually about the simplest things played to the highest level.

I know you bought this book for insights and life lessons in how to build your career and practising might seem like something for real beginners, but this is so, so, so important. Please don't overlook this part of the book or underestimate just how vital it is.

> *When it comes to marketing yourself, practice is the biggest short-cut in the whole book.*

Being the best drummer in your college or the top guitarist in your village is an achievement, but when it comes to achieving real success we are talking about being able to compete with the rest of the world.

Part Two: Song Writing

This part of the book is here to help you understand the difference between a professional songwriter and someone who's just writing for a hobby. While there are many famous songwriters, such as Skrillex and Diplo, who've written for the likes of Justin Bieber and Missy Elliot and have won Grammy awards, these people are at the very top of their game and will have worked really hard to get there. Most songwriters reading this book will have been writing songs with no professional feedback at all and doing whatever they want to.

> *While creativity is key, if you want to become a published songwriter you always have to keep at the forefront of your mind that you're not just writing for yourself, you're writing for other people.*

If you want to take this to the next level you have to have an audience buy into what you do. This part of the book will help you do this and get you thinking and acting like a professional songwriter.

Top line melodies

Every day I get sent 50+ demo albums or tracks from bands all over the world and one thing that consistently lets them down is the top line melody. The top line melody is the thing that people are going to hum along to, the recognisable part of the song. It's really important that it's strong, so why not get help with it? Why not bring in a top line melody writer? Not to write the whole song for you but someone who can say, 'Do you think we can make the chorus more of a hook?' Or, 'Do you think we can make the chorus bigger via the top line melody?' Having someone help you structure the top line melody could make all the difference because, don't forget, you're only ever one song away from world domination.

Top line melodies can become very difficult to write because of the arrangement within the song. A lot of the time bands will create a complicated structure, with the bass, guitar and drums all doing their own thing, placing real limitations on the melody. So often it's not just about coming up with a melody, it's about clearing the way for the melody because the arrangement is too complicated. For more on this, see the section on arrangements.

Auto-Tune

Musicians often have set ideas about what is cheating and what's acceptable and therefore success is about doing things in a very specific way with very specific rules in order to make it credible. One of those rules is to not use Auto-Tune. Well, I'm here to tell you that I think it's fine to break this rule. The reality is, not everyone can sing perfectly every time and singing in a studio can be a very different ball game to singing live. Auto-Tune isn't a cheat, it's just a tool to help you sound as good as you possibly can and save you time. Don't fight it. If you're a technically phenomenal singer who doesn't need it, fantastic, but the fact is, some of the biggest bands of all time haven't necessarily had the most technical singers. It's important to recognise that not everyone is great in a studio and if that's the case for you, Auto-Tune can really help.

Lyrics and subject matter

It doesn't matter if you're Andrew WK and you want to party all day or you're Rage Against the Machine and you want to take down the system, what matters is how you convey your message to your audience. I see far too many lyrics that are haphazard and don't really mean anything. If you feel this is true for you why not bring someone in who can look at your lyrics and give you some expert advice, pointing out if a line is too cheesy, or could be made better or stronger. Again, I'm not talking about someone writing the lyrics for you but more holding you accountable to what you're putting down because your audience will notice and it does matter. You have to make your lyrics mean something. It's important to realise that you don't have to control every aspect of your music career, it's OK to sometimes relinquish control to the hands of an expert, especially if professional success is what you're after. Seeking help and advice with your lyrics will lead to real improvement.

Stealing

I need to clarify right up front that when I say stealing what I really mean is using your favourite bands for inspiration rather than plagiarising another musician. Take ideas that you love and put your own unique spin on them. I've done this with almost every business I've started. I've seen something I like and I've taken that model and changed certain aspects of it to improve upon it and make it more me. BIMM was a great example of this. Basically it was a cooler version of ACM – the college we'd built before – it wasn't an original idea. When I set up my music management company we took the original model for covers bands and streamlined and modernised it. Whereas before everyone was playing in bad suits, looking like the traditional 'functions band', we gave people a band that looked as if they should be on the front cover of NME, that looked like a real band instead of a wedding band. We made the songs they played more current too. Now everyone does this, but at the time it was revolutionary.

When it comes to songs, taking inspiration from a certain drum groove or guitar line is part and parcel of today's music world because everything's been done to death. You need to find the line between inspiration and plagiarism in order to create great art. Figure out what you love about other people's songs and implement it into your own unique work.

Arrangements

The trouble with having three or more people working on songs is that everyone will want to get their own way and they can end up becoming a mishmash of ideas that aren't necessarily in the best interests of the song, which can also end up being five to six minutes long. In inexperienced bands, everybody wants to put their stamp on a song, but if you're adding complicated parts to other complicated parts you'll make the track very hard to listen to and it will be difficult for the singer to add in a melody (see earlier section on top line melodies). This is where it can be hugely beneficial to enlist the help of an arranger, to take an objective overview and say things like, 'No you can't have a guitar solo there' or 'No, you can't have this drum fill or put these extra strings in.'

> *In most hit records the parts are minimal, so having someone who can step back and simplify everything is key.*

I'm not a songwriter, but I can tell you what works and what doesn't and one of the most common problems I find with songs is that they're far too complicated. Having someone come in and objectively tell you what's working and what isn't will also help alleviate arguing within the band. I can't stress enough how important arrangement is, especially if you want to get on the radio. Things like the vocals coming in straight away really matter.

Song writing lessons

As I've previously mentioned, in the sport world it doesn't matter what level an athlete is at, they will have a coach. That coach doesn't have to be as good as them athletically but they play a vital role spurring them on to get better. The same applies in the music world. If you want to be the best songwriter you can be you need some kind of regular coaching. Try finding writers in your local area to help keep you accountable and keep you upping your game. The fact is, if you're writing something that you know someone will be looking at in a critical way you'll try harder. If you're only writing when you feel like it you won't improve and you'll just keep doing the same old, same old. You need someone to push you out of your comfort zone and try new things. Comfort zones might be rooted in fear, but fear can also help us improve, if we choose to let it.

I'd also recommend you spend time practising song-writing the same way you would practise with an instrument. Set yourself targets and goals. Search online for tips and lessons, so you're constantly improving and not just coasting along doing whatever you want whenever you want.

Part Three: Rehearsing

In my experience, most bands are frustrated with where they're at, and would like to progress their music career faster. But if you analyse what most bands do you'll see why they get stuck in a rut. Maybe this sounds familiar to you: You start a new band and it's very exciting, you start writing songs and rehearsing, you put out an EP that doesn't go very far, you do a bunch of gigs, the first few are great but over time it becomes harder to get friends, family and your audience to attend, the band gets bored, someone leaves, the band breaks up and you're back to square one. So often, the reason for this happening is that bands don't set themselves up to succeed, they set themselves up to fail.

So, how do you set yourself up to succeed? In my opinion, it's all in the rehearsals. Rehearsals are the engine room when it comes to being a musician. They encompass every aspect of learning, from looking after your audience to experimenting, creativity, delivery and marketing. Even planning and products fall under the rehearsals umbrella because so often they're where you write new songs. As rehearsals are so important they need to be set up in the most productive, efficient way possible, and this is where so many musicians fall down.

Do you recognise this scenario? You turn up to the rehearsal room and someone's usually late and someone else has got a few tinnies. You spend the first ten minutes chatting about everyone's week and what they've been watching on Netflix. Then you do a rough sound check to make sure the levels are OK, before spending the remainder of the rehearsal playing through some songs, then patting each other on the back and leaving it another week until the next rehearsal. I'm willing to bet that scenario describes 80% of all bands in the world.

This section of the book is all about how to set yourself up to succeed by getting the most from every aspect of your rehearsals, including song writing, set construction, performance targets, time management and priority management.

Planning your rehearsal

Most bands that I come into contact with don't set a target for their rehearsals and personally, I think this is a huge mistake. Before you set foot in the rehearsal room, you should decide what you are going to rehearse and what you want the outcome of your rehearsal to be. For example, if you've got a new member in the band, you need to have a general rehearsal to make sure that everyone knows the songs. But once the band know their parts and are tight, you'll be able to rehearse for a more specific reason, like for a show.

A performance rehearsal is very different to a general rehearsal, which we'll come on to soon. Another, more specific type of rehearsal is a creative rehearsal, where the focus is on song-writing. Whatever the type of rehearsal, there needs to be a goal, for example, to finish writing a song, and the more specific you are with that goal, the better. Imagine if you went into a rehearsal with the goal of constructing the best set list, rather than writing one five minutes before you go on stage. All of a sudden the focus will be on the intros and endings and whether the tempos and lyrical content fit together. You won't need to rehearse the entire songs.

Another benefit of planning rehearsals and their goals is that people arriving late or bringing tinnies will no longer be acceptable. By knowing what you need to achieve and sending these objectives to your band members beforehand, you're setting a higher level of expectation. This is where it can really help to appoint a musical director. An MD's job is to manage the time, targets, achievements and people in a rehearsal and make sure you all get the most from it. Usually the MD is the most experienced person in the band, preferably a multi-instrumentalist, who can communicate with the drummer as well as the guitarist or bass player. A lot of MDs are keyboard players because their theoretical knowledge is high but it's more important to have someone who is a natural communicator and facilitator to drive things forward. It also needs to be someone with good organisational skills.

Breaking songs down to make them tight

Usually in rehearsals, people turn up – and more often than not late, don't get me started on that – plug in and start playing. But I'm a firm believer in breaking things down first and going back to basics. To get the most from your rehearsals you need to dissect each track into its different parts – the intro, verses, chorus and middle eight. You need to break it down in terms of instruments too, always starting with the drums because if they aren't right from the start, it's a lot harder to fix them later. Analyse the time, power and consistency, then you can add in the bass. When it comes to the bass I'd mostly be looking at feel, and making sure the bass player sits in the pocket of the groove (see *The art of simplicity* in the *Practising* section).

Then I'd look at the melodic content, from the guitars and keyboards etc, focusing on the timing, feel and frequencies. Lots of bands will try to replicate the sound of a track made in the studio, which might have ten different guitar parts and sounds layered on top of each other. But this will be difficult if you've only got one guitar when you're playing live, so spend time on parts, chord structure and tonality. The most important thing is being able to hear what the vocalist sings; if there's a clash of frequencies it will be very difficult to hear them. Breaking things down like this enables you to start making space in each song for the different frequencies.

> *So, to summarise, the jigsaw pieces of a rehearsal should go:*
> *drums, bass, guitar, keyboard, vocals.*

I would do this at every rehearsal to get things as tight as possible and I would always break a track down if something doesn't sound right. The reason bands don't do this is because it's boring for the musicians who have to sit around and wait to play. But ultimately, it all comes down to how badly you want to improve and succeed.

As I said at the start of this section, it's not just about breaking things down in terms of instruments but also in terms of the different parts of a song and how they lead into each other. Often, when you're transitioning from a verse to the chorus there will be a sense of excitement and the tendency to speed up slightly, which makes the track feel less powerful. Personally, I'd always have a click set up in the rehearsal room. Having the backbone of a click to work with is crucial when it comes to finding the perfect tempo. At some point I'd rehearse the transition from verse to chorus over and over, just as I would re-hearse the whole track. I would also spend time looping a section like a verse around and around so that it sits nicely in the groove without any transition. Breaking it down structurally like this will make sure it sounds as tight as pos-sible. Most bands don't do this but when you're being paid to work as a ses-sion player or going into a studio with a producer these kind of details will be looked at.

Rehearsing the show not the songs

Does this scenario sound familiar? After your weekly rehearsals, a gig comes in and you start deciding what tracks you're going to put into the set backstage or in the van on the way. Then, when you perform the show, the front person either announces every song or looks around at you, waiting awkwardly for the song to start. Something I hear musicians say all the time is 'when I'm on stage I really go for it'. This might be true for the first few minutes but then I see the energy drop. Often this is because they haven't had a performance rehearsal.

A lot of bands avoid rehearsing for a show as opposed to simply rehearsing songs, because it's embarrassing and hard. But doing so enables you to avoid so many pitfalls once you're on stage. Let me give you an example: When playing live, guitarists will want to change their guitar after certain songs. There's nothing wrong with that but when a guitarist makes a change it takes at least 20 to 30 seconds, or maybe even a minute (unless you have a guitar-tech walking on with your guitar, which I'm assuming you don't). What happens during that time if you haven't planned for it? Nothing. And standing on stage doing nothing for 30 seconds while the audience are staring up at you can feel like an eternity. All you can think is, *please God start the song!* In a performance rehearsal you can plan what to do to bypass this awkwardness. You can get clear on which songs will need guitar changes, and you can decide how to keep the audience's attention. For example, the front person saying something, or the rhythm section starting the song without the guitarist to keep the energy going. Either way, something is planned to keep up the momentum. Personally, I want to know everything that's going to happen on a gig so that I can plan what I'll be doing and where I'll be. I love performance rehearsals because they don't leave anything to chance.

Another thing to bear in mind at your performance rehearsals are the messages you want to get across to the audience. I know this can be hugely embarrassing to practise but it enables the rest of the band to see how long they've got in between each track. It also stops any cheesy rambling. Get clear on the statements you want to make beforehand, as opposed to making stuff up as you go along on the night, which can be hard for the audience to follow. I want the front person to inject energy into the crowd with a 'thank you' or 'are you ready to have some fun tonight?' and less of the 'a funny thing happened on the way to the gig'. Performance rehearsals build confidence within the band and you'll also blow away every other band on the bill because you'll have a show that looks professionally put together rather than an ad hoc playlist. And remember, even though it's embarrassing practising these kind of things in the rehearsal room, it's a hell of a lot more embarrassing when things go wrong on stage!

The marketing opportunity

Every single week without fail musicians will ask me what content I think they ought to put on their social media. I always advise them to use their socials to tell their stories and news and document what they do. Rehearsals provide a massive opportunity to market your band in this way because everyone is together with their instruments and able to do something interesting, exciting and emotion-driven. And the best thing about using your rehearsals as a marketing opportunity is that it's free.

You could post a band picture, perform something, do a live Q&A, or a giveaway. Rehearsals offer the perfect opportunity to do something creative for your audience, whilst telling a story and building a bit of excitement. Plan what you're going to do social media wise ahead of your rehearsal. Work out how you can make the most of the opportunity and give your followers the most value. Don't leave all of your social media content for your live performances. Everyone loves the behind the scenes stories. As marketers, bands tend to be obsessed with what they're doing rather than *why* they're doing it. But the why is what the audience will buy into. You have the opportunity to tell the story of why you're rehearsing, in a very exciting way. For example, you could share with your audience that you're going to be performing a new track. You could tell them the story behind that track, or play them a snippet.

Rehearsals are full of opportunities for fun as well. You could do a Facebook or Insta Live for the last 10 to 15 minutes and play requests from your audience. If you focus on having fun it will negate the fact that it might not sound very good. It all adds to the social currency of the fans who are involved because they'll know more about the band than the other fans, whether that's what songs you're playing in the set, in which order, or being in on the in-jokes from the band members.

In 2017 Metallica treated their fans to a live stream of a rehearsal for their up-coming WorldWired tour. A few days before, a message appeared on the band's Facebook page saying, '*To kick off the celebrations, we're inviting you to get a sneak peak of what to expect this summer by checking out our rehearsal the night before the first show via the magic of streaming video on Facebook Live. In a little show very cleverly titled "Now That We're Live" we'll bring rehearsals on Tuesday, May 9 live to your computer, tablet, mobile device or any other way you reach the internet.*'

As a fan of the band I was really excited to see the guys in rehearsal and my head was full of questions like, *what does a Metallica rehearsal look like? Can Lars still play?* And of course, *will there be a fight?* It shows that even the biggest bands in the world are using live streams and social media to bring their audience value.

Record and document your rehearsal

How many times do you make decisions in a rehearsal with your band only for it to be completely forgotten about by the following week? Two things I always take into a rehearsal are a pad to take notes and a fully charged phone to record video or voice notes, so that I can document what I'm doing. By documenting your rehearsals you can make sure that every decision is seen through, and this is crucial. It's so hard to remember little tweaks made to a song. Times that by twenty different tweaks in an average rehearsal and it shows why bands don't progress very much. Documenting also helps you be accountable for your next rehearsal. The other things it does is allow you to see the growth of the band. You're able to practise things and compare them at different dates. Imagine if you did three different set lists and recorded them so you could watch them back in entirety to see what works and doesn't.

There have been so many times when I've watched a recording of my band rehearse and I've realised that we've been playing too fast because we've got carried away trying to get the energy levels up. It's very difficult to notice these things when you're in the moment. The next day you're able to analyse your rehearsal and things like the guitar sound, drum fill or the tempo more objectively.

> *This is how every sportsman or woman improves their game. They will watch recordings of their performances to see where and how they need to improve.*

Musicians need to implement this same level of thoroughness and professionalism if they want to improve. Buy a small gorilla grip for your phone so that you can just put it in a corner and record. Or have each band member record themselves. Having recordings of your rehearsals also really helps if you need to draft another musician in. You can simply show them what it is that you do.

The etiquette of rehearsals

Appointing a musical director is a great way of getting the most from your rehearsals. First and foremost, an MD should be a facilitator, not a dictator, there to oversee and encourage each member of the band to speak. I've had my fair share of dictator MDs in rehearsals and usually the band suffers for it because they'll only be working to one person's way of doing things. A good MD is about getting every band member involved and pooling their combined expertise. They will also ensure that it doesn't turn into a free for all and help avoid arguments or scenarios where band members are too scared to say anything. It can be tough to communicate in a band rehearsal because there's a lot of noise and a lot of people in the room. When you get four or more musicians with their instruments in their hands they're going to want to play something. Stopping and starting on cue is so important. It's very frustrating when you try to stop a musician and they keep playing for six bars. You only have a set amount of time in rehearsals and so much time is wasted trying to get people to stop playing. It's important to have and adhere to certain signals that dictate when people need to stop. When you're rehearsing to get things tight, have everyone stand close together in a circle with a clear signal that means stop, so it's easier to communicate and take cues from each other.

Starting can be a problem too. Everyone should be ready to play at all times, so that when someone says 'play' you're good to go. Some other rules of rehearsal etiquette are as follows: Drummers shouldn't play while guitarists tune. Guitarists shouldn't noodle while everyone else is talking. Drummers, for the love of God, please don't take the top of your hi-hat off the stand, tighten it up and put it back on again AFTER EVERY SONG! If it needs tightening every 30 seconds get a better one. Just bring the gear you need. Guitarists, don't bring every pedal that's ever been invented when you're only going to use three. The more things you've got that *can* go wrong, the more *will* go wrong. Think of it like a bank robbery. Your job is to get in, get the job done and get out as quickly as possible.

Unless you're rehearsing for a show, your job is to maximise the time you're paying for. A lot of the gear you need will be there already, so you bring the breakables – like guitars, bass, cymbals and bass drum pedal. Rehearsal rooms will have things like amps. Get in and set up as quickly as possible. Don't waste time on chat. Don't turn up late or with wrong or faulty or too much gear – these are all cardinal sins. However, the biggest sin of all is musicians not learning their parts / songs properly. You must know the frustration of standing in a rehearsal room while one of the other musicians is asking you what the chords are. For me, this is a sackable offence for the continual offender as it's the most basic thing. If a musician turns up to a rehearsal and they haven't thoroughly learnt their parts they are either not good enough or don't want it badly enough. Either way it should be a red flag!

Set list construction

Set list construction is a subject very close to my heart. I believe that it's an art form and, just as you'd spend hours practising on your instrument and playing live, I'd put a long, long time into practising set list construction. It's not just about putting the right songs in the right order, it's about creating a show. When it comes to choosing your first song you need to start as strong as you can and hold nothing back. Do something so good that people will tell any latecomers they've missed something great. Don't save your biggest song till last until you're at the level where people are paying money to see you.

If you don't have the perfect song to open the show then why not write one? *Let Me Entertain You* by Robbie Williams is a great example of this. It's clear from the lyrical content, the tempo, the arrangement, the build up at the beginning, the huge chorus and the massive outro that they wrote it to be a set-opener. When Robbie Williams finishes that song he has the audience eating out of the palm of his hand and it's all plain sailing from there.

Other points to bear in mind when constructing your set list are what the front man's going to say and when and where the guitar changes are going to be. Don't have a change after a powerful moment, as you'll need to keep the momentum going. In terms of energy, I would start massively high and keep it building for at least two or three songs.

Bands always want to play for too long. If you're gigging on the local circuit I'd advise you make your set no more than 25 minutes. Go on, smash it up, and leave people wanting more. Just because you can play for longer it doesn't mean you should. And I'd recommend you only have one slow song – unless of course you're a crooner and slow songs are your thing. Usually though, people are there for a party, to jump up and down and sing along.

Just as some songs should only go at the beginning of a show, others are clearly written for the end. If you put *New York New York* in the middle of your set the audience won't know what to do. You should also avoid having more than one or two end songs in a row. It will be too emotionally draining for your audience, a bit like watching *The Lord of the Rings* when you keep thinking that it's finished but it hasn't.

If you don't have a good end song I would definitely advise that you write one. You need to leave your audience on a high, thinking your set was absolutely fantastic. People tend to remember the opening and closing minutes to a set the most, and how they made them feel. You want to leave them feeling super-charged. Encourage participation in your last song but make sure that it doesn't drag on too. The audience will be looking for a clear cue that your set is over, don't do anything to confuse them.

I really believe that set list construction is an art form. Study what works and doesn't from other bands. Look at the tempos of the songs they choose and how they link them. Bands like Queen offer a masterclass in transitions, and you will see that everything, such as Freddie Mercury singing 'day-oh', has its carefully chosen place.

When I structure a set list I usually print the songs out then cut them up individually with a scissors. Then I place them on a table and start moving them around. This way I can visualise what the tracks will look like while I'm thinking about tempos, intros and endings, guitar changes etc.

Set lists differ from gig to gig and how long you will be performing for, but whether it's 30 minutes, 60 minutes or two hours, there are key times in the set where the audience needs to be directed. Below is my recommended format for a set list and, as they can be different lengths, I have split them into percentages.

- ***The opener***
  For the first two or three songs you are going to show the audience what you've got in store for them and you are going to start strong, like a metaphorical punch in the face. If it can be bigger and better then do it. You're not there to build up to something. This is a fight to show how good you are right from the start because first impressions count!

- ***Time to change things up a bit***
  Next, we have a chance for the front person to talk briefly. I would think about having a change in tempo or even a shuffle groove, so things don't become too one dimensional.

- ***Ballad***
  A ballad should come into the set about two thirds of the way through to bring the vibe down and allow the audience a chance to breathe before you take it back up a notch.

- ***Big hitters***
  If this were a boxing match, now's the time to line up some combos that will knock your audience to the floor. It's time to bring out some big hitters. The next song should show the audience that you're planning a powerful end to the gig. And your last song is your chance to finish things off before the final bell – if you've got your set list right, at this point the knees will be wobbly!

- ***The encore***
  It's time to put things to bed and make sure this audience doesn't forget your performance. The fighter is off the canvas and it's lights out time! Load up and end in style or, to quote the great Duke Evers in *Rocky IV*, 'All your strength, all your power, all your love. Everything you have got. Right now!'

Part Four: Performing

Gigging is the aspect of music that I have the most experience in. I've been doing well over 100 gigs per year for twenty years so, having done over 2,000 gigs in total, there's not a lot that throws me when it comes to playing live. I don't get nervous when I perform, unless I'm unprepared or caught off guard by being thrown into a situation that I feel uncomfortable with. If I ever have to perform a track I haven't had a chance to learn properly, or if someone expects me to change the key unexpectedly, or if I'm performing with musicians that I don't feel are up to the task, then I get nervous. In this section I'm going to highlight some of the key pitfalls you can encounter when it comes to gigging, so that in the future you can do your best to avoid them, or at least be prepared.

Who are you?

The question *'who are you?'* applies all the way through the gig, from how you perform to how you market yourself. Everything you do is being judged, not just the music. Being aware of this from the moment you turn up until you leave is crucial. So, whether it's to a promoter, a client, another band or in front of the audience, how you act is crucial.

> *When you're performing, everybody needs to know who you are.*

There are many different ways you can let them know. You could have the band name on the bass drum or a backdrop or banners down the side of the stage. You could hand out business cards or flyers and the front person could regularly announce the band name and where you can be found online. I've lost count of the number of gigs I've been to where I've really been enjoying a band's set but have no clue who they are because the singer hasn't said and there's been no on-stage marketing. You can't ask anyone because it's so noisy and by the time the next band's playing the chances are I'll have forgotten about them and they'll have missed a trick.

This is down to bad planning. I'd rather have the name of my band all over the place and repeated throughout the set than leave the audience with no clue. I do this with all of our bands at DK Management. It's really important that people know who our bands are so they can find and follow them and hopefully book them for another gig. It's all about building brand awareness. Even quite large bands will probably have people in the audience who don't know who they are.

Who you are isn't all about your name though. Through your songs and your performance you're also showing the audience what you stand for. Everything that's good and bad about you will be transparent on a gig, so your job is to make sure that everyone knows who you are for the right reasons.

Gig etiquette

Gig etiquette is so important when it comes to getting gigs from gigs. In the covers band world a good band will gig 50 times a year. If they're doing 70 gigs a year there's something special about them. If they get to 100 gigs in a year they've done everything right because it means they're even getting offered gigs in the quiet times like January and February and on the 'off-peak' days like Monday or Thursday. My band, The Indie Killers, did 140 gigs last year, which as a hobby, was very difficult to fit in! The reason we got so many gigs was because we paid attention to etiquette at every stage of the process, from the moment we contacted the clients, to the way we dealt with the venue, performed on the night, and promoted ourselves. You have to pay attention to every detail to get this number of gigs.

The weird thing about writing this book is that I'm having to stop myself saying the word 'value' on almost every page. Maybe I should have called it 'The value of Value!'

> *Every time I start a business, a band or any other project the question I'm searching to answer is "where is the value I can provide?"*

The answer so often lies in making other people's lives easier and etiquette is the simplest way to make this difference. You can do it for free and it's so easy to go that extra mile for whoever you are working with.

The first few years I was playing in bands I noticed a trend. So many musicians weren't willing to compromise their art, which is admirable when you are putting out your first album. However, when musicians aren't willing to compromise over whether their band can fit into a small space at a wedding gig or if sandwiches are OK instead of a hot meal they need to think of the bigger picture and not be a diva. One of my biggest pet peeves is musicians bitching about having to eat sandwiches on a gig. For fuck's sake, you're a grown up, so sort some food out before you get there – unless you need your mum to cook for you! Gigs are won and lost by making other people's lives as easy as possible and the divas don't last long in this business.

If you're playing in an originals band you never know where the people you're working with will end up or how successful they might become. You also don't know how helpful their friends and family could be at spreading the word. So the next time you don't watch another band because you've got better things to do, or the next time you don't bring as many people as you'd told the promoter you would, just be aware that word spreads and people have long memories. Another no-no when it comes to gig etiquette is performing too long past your allocated slot. Ditto going off into the crowd to see your friends after you've played. This really annoys the venue because they want you to get your stuff off stage so they can go home. Everything you do affects how your band and your brand is perceived.

Another really important final note on etiquette is to play for the audience not for yourself. Play the songs that they will want to hear. Remember, value! Value! VALUE!

How to front a band

Fronting a band is an absolute art form. Your front person is the gel that holds everything together and the tour guide for the night. A front person can take a gig from good to world class, from a disaster to acceptable. The front person is also the one who gets people to do the things you want them to, such as buying your merch, or following your socials. You don't need to shout to do this but you do need to be engaging. There has to be something about you that gets people's attention. If you think about what makes the best front people it's not what they say but the energy behind it and how they say it. Freddie Mercury was one of the greatest examples of this of all time. He could hold an audience in the palm of his hand by the way he moved and talked, as a well his singing. I also believe that Robbie Williams' fronting ability transformed him from an average boy band singer to a world class artist. There's very few people who can command an audience without saying a word. To be able to do this you need presence and authority.

If you're fronting a band here are some tips: Firstly, only talk when you need to talk. For example, when there's a guitar change, or once you're three or four songs in and the audience will be expecting you to say something.

Secondly, don't chat, make statements. When you're in a venue there's a lot of background noise from people talking or cheering or from the noise on stage. If you're chatting it's very difficult for the audience to understand what you're saying and it's very easy for the energy of the gig to drop off as a result. Say things in short bursts like 'make some noise' or 'is everyone having a good time?' That way, you're opening communication with the audience and providing them with a burst of energy.

Of course, the way you talk to your audience will depend on your genre of music. Norah Jones is going to be a very different front person to Billy Joe from Green Day. She'll be guiding her audience through the night, telling stories and making it personal, while Billie Joe's agenda is to whip the crowd into a frenzy.

I would aim to say the band name three times over the course of a gig, at the beginning, middle and end. I'd also tell them where to find you online. And don't forget your calls to action if you've got a new single out or you want them to go to your website or listen to something or do something. Make you call to action at the end of your set when you say thank you.

Try to avoid being funny unless it's something you've prepared, because musicians aren't comedians and it can come across as awkward, especially when off the cuff. And always have something prepared to say in an unexpected break, for example if the snare drum goes or a guitar string breaks.

If you're not the front person, make sure that whoever's fronting your band knows when the breaks are going to be. If you're a guitarist, let them know when you plan to change your guitars so they can plan accordingly.

Stage presence

When you're starting out as a musician your inexperience can be all too apparent. One of the best ways to overcome this is through your stage presence. Where your band stand on stage and how they move and perform gives the game away when it comes to confidence. The fact is, you're there to perform. If people just wanted to listen to your music they'd stick it on Spotify. Therefore the audience is the most important part of the show and everything should be directed towards them. When a bass player spends the gig facing the drummer it shows a lack of confidence and a lack of excitement or energy. Fretboard staring or pedalboard gazing is dull and uninteresting to watch and therefore these things should be second nature and part of the rehearsals before gigs. Remember when I said you should practice things until you can't do them wrong? Well, that goes for pedals too, so your attention can be where it's needed – on the audience.

> *Standing at the front of the stage fully facing the crowd with your head up will give the audience confidence, because confidence is infectious, as is nervousness.*

It feels so awkward for the audience if it becomes apparent that the

42

band are scared. Eye contact is really important. Musicians have a tendency to look at their fret boards or hands as a safety mechanism, but if you do this you aren't fully engaging with your audience. And if you need to do this in order to play correctly you haven't learned your songs well enough!

One of the first things I do when I'm performing is to look across at one of my bandmates within the first 30 seconds and give them the biggest grin because that will inspire confidence in them. I want the musicians I'm playing with to know that I am 100% in control and they don't have anything to worry about. It's nice for the audience to see that going on within the band too and the confidence spreads very quickly.

When it comes to moving around on stage, know your surroundings. Whatever the size of the stage, there will be different problems to overcome. When you play on a small stage you don't want to smash the singer in the face with your headstock. But when you play on a massive stage you've got a lot of space to fill. The key is to perform according to your surroundings. When you're playing in a tight space making eye contact with your audience is really important – it's a key way of showing your energy to them because you can't move around much. If you're performing on a big stage, make sure you get your sound right, as you might be away from your amp for a while. And know that when you're on a big stage you have a lot more room to cover and you need to cover it. You need to be the master of that space, you can't wilt away into the background.

When I moved away to go to music college I was determined to pay my way via my bass playing and I'd play anywhere, anytime to earn money. While in a covers duo with one of my mates on the course, we landed a contract to play on the ferry from Dover, UK to Calais, France. The 20 mile journey would take 90 minutes and every weekend we would travel backwards and forwards over 20 times a day as we weren't allowed off the boat. Our job was to play for six of those crossings, for an hour each session. Most days we would get bored and end up playing nine or ten hours a day until we lost our voices or our fingers were too sore but it was more fun than the sea sickness and staff cabins. The stage was 6ft by 4ft and we got the gig because there were only two of us (guitar, bass and backing track). Even though we were only a duo, we still didn't fit onto the stage properly and on rough crossings we'd end up bumping each other off the stage completely. It was ridiculous but we loved it and were thankful to get paid to play. We were just two guys who wanted to play music and have fun, and as a result, Christian, the other guy in the duo, is one of the best guitarists I have ever seen.

What to wear on stage

I don't understand why so many bands don't co-ordinate what they're going to wear when they're on stage. So often, they don't match at all. For example, you get a guy wearing a surf t-shirt in a heavy metal band, or the outfits are exactly the same, which can look even weirder. What you wear when you perform is so important, especially if you're the front person. A lot of musicians think that it's cool to not make much of an effort with their appearance, not realising that a lot of massive artists go to a hell of a lot of effort to make it *look* as if they *didn't* make an effort. Liam Gallagher from Oasis is a good example of this. You can still wear jeans and a t-shirt but it's got to be the right jeans and t-shirt, à la Justin Timberlake. They need to be well thought out and specifically chosen to go together.

Another big bugbear of mine are fungus-beards. A fungus-beard is a '*haven't made an effort*' beard; the patchy kind of facial hair that looks more like you've got pubes on your face as opposed to a really great *beard*-beard. The same rule applies with haircuts. The music industry is a fashion-led industry, whether you like it or not. Walking on stage with a £5 haircut that looks like it was done by your mum is not going to cut it, excuse the pun.

Another thing to be wary of is wearing all black. There's a common assumption that wearing black on stage is the done thing but you need to be careful that you don't look like a member of the crew – or a floating head if the backdrop is black too.

What if, like me, you are not into fashion? Find someone to help you and your band. You don't have to pay for a stylist. You could approach a local college and find a really cool fashion student to help advise you on your look. To be honest with you, I genuinely couldn't give a shit about what I wear but I know that if I want to stand out and get attention, I have to get my girlfriend, Ella, to help me because she's got an eye for what looks good and I haven't. Every time I've been in a band I've got outside help with what to wear on stage. Handing over the responsibility to someone else leaves you free to focus on the music.

Like I said before, it's important that you and your band members don't wear identical outfits but there does need to be some kind of theme. And I would say that this applies to how you look when you turn up at a gig, as well as when you're on stage. You don't need to wear your gig clothes but it helps to look like a rock star rather than a scruffy student.

The pace of the gig

Pace is all about how you string everything together as a show, as opposed to just performing a random bunch of songs.

> *Getting the pace right is crucial and plays a huge part in separating you from local level bands and putting you in the national league.*

Think of your show like running a marathon. If you start too fast it can break the pace, and the same applies if you start too slow. You definitely need to hit the ground running but you also need to keep your audience excited from the first moment till the last.

As soon as the drummer first clicks his sticks into a gig it's effectively the start of the race and you're setting the pace with that first song. You're not just setting the pace in terms of speed, you're setting the energy level, and that's what really matters. The energy has to be at the right level. Usually a band will play their songs a little bit faster at a gig than on a record to make it feel more exciting. From there, every decision you make will affect the pace of the energy. If the gaps between songs are too long or too short they're interrupting the flow. It's up to the drummer to find the sweet spot between one song ending and the next beginning. Leave it too long and vibe starts to die, too soon and the audience won't be ready and it'll be a shock to the system. Lastly, if there are going to be any breaks in your show, make sure you know who's responsible for keeping the energy at the right pace.

The same applies with the tempos of each song and how you ebb and flow between them. Don't think that the tempo has to be relentlessly upbeat to maintain the energy. I once saw Damien Rice perform at the Royal Albert Hall in London and about two thirds of the way through the gig he unplugged his guitar, walked away from the mic and sang *Cannon Ball*. The acoustics in Albert Hall are phenomenal and the energy was incredible and no-one made a noise or moved a muscle. It was like watching the World Snooker final, absolutely electric, despite being completely unplugged! Which just goes to show that pace isn't always about tempo, it's about keeping the energy alive throughout the gig.

Anything which could interrupt the pace of the gig needs to be highlighted. For instance, if a guitar needs to be tuned or if the singer is going to pick up an instrument, it has to be part of the story of the show to keep the energy from waning. In summary, it's all about how you make your show one coherent piece as opposed to lots of individual parts.

When it all goes wrong

I've had some amazing experiences in the 2,000-plus gigs I've done in my life, but I've also had many occasions when things have gone wrong. One thing I've learned is that, although you sometimes can't control things going wrong, you can control how you deal with it. And it's how you deal with it as a group that really matters. Times of crisis can really bond a band together like a family. Let me give you some examples of how things have gone wrong for me...

I once ran out on stage in front of 40,000 people at a festival when it had been raining and the stage was wet. When I came to my spot the top half of my body stopped but my legs kept sliding and I hit the floor heavier than the entire line up of Download festival! As I fell, I heard the crowd roar 'wahey!' While I was embarrassed, I laughed it off, got up and started playing.

Another time, my band did a gig on a boat and we had to take all of our gear across on a plank. A very narrow plank. This unnerved the singer and she had a wobble, accidentally throwing our mixing desk into the Thames. We all watched, mouths open and hearts sinking, knowing that we wouldn't be able to play without it. But again, we stayed calm in a crisis and all got on the phone and our socials, asking everyone we knew in the vicinity if they could lend us a mixer as an emergency. Thankfully, we managed to pull it off.

Now let me tell you about the worst gig of my entire life. My band and I were still young, based in Wales and trying to build a reputation in England. One day we got offered a gig in London by an agent. It was a last minute gig and the sound man said not to bring a PA as he had one. When we got there we discovered that his idea of a PA was basically a record player, two wheels of steel decks. We had to try and find a PA from somewhere – and fast – but we didn't know anyone in England. And sadly, this was only the beginning. At that moment, someone tested the strobe light and the sound man had an epileptic fit, fell over and hit his head on the desk. As his head made contact with the desk it made that terrible cracking sound where you think, *there's no coming back from that, he's dead.* Thankfully, he didn't die, but he did need to be rushed to hospital in an ambulance. So now we had no PA or sound man. We finally located a colossal PA in another part of the venue but none of us had a clue how to work it. Needless to say, the gig was an absolute shit show. But it gets worse. At the end of the night we went up to venue owner to get paid and he told us that he didn't pay on the night. I thought he was pulling a fast one because the gig had been shit and I came from a background where you often got fleeced by venues. So I started putting pressure on him to pay us. A little too much pressure as it turns out. The police got called and they arrested me and took the whole band to the station. Once I'd explained what had happened they were very nice and let me go. But still it gets worse, because I'd left my guitar at the venue! I had to get a taxi back there at 2am and grovel to the guy to get it back. Finally, he returned it and the band and I began the long drive home. Not a word was spoken on that journey back. I think we were all contemplating whether we ought to throw in the towel and become accountants – or in my case, a debt collector!

When things go wrong it comes down to your problem-solving skills. I'm only good at solving problems now because I've had so many to try and solve in the years I've been playing. Don't be too hard on yourself if and when the crap hits the fan. Know that it's helping you in the long run. And it's far better that you learn what to do when you're just starting out and playing smaller venues than cocking things up in a stadium. One thing I always say to the musicians at DK Management is that it's easy when things go right. You really earn your money when it all goes wrong because then it's brown trousers time. Don't be afraid of messing things up though, it's all invaluable experience.

Part Five: Touring

Life on the road is most musicians' idea of a perfect life and it really can be a privilege. I'll never forget the time touring took me to Poland and I woke up in a castle overlooking Krakow. Or the times I got to hang out backstage with Taylor Hawkins, the second best drummer in the Foo Fighters, chatting about life and music. However, beneath the romance and glamour of life on the road comes a harsh reality – it's an incredibly tough lifestyle to maintain over a period of years, mentally draining as well as physically. In this section of the book we're going to meet these challenges head on and I'll share my tips for dealing with them, so that you'll be able to enjoy all the good stuff that comes with being a musician.

Eating and staying healthy

If you're going to go on gigs two or three times a week, you're choosing a life where you'll regularly be getting in at three or four in the morning. You'll also be spending a large proportion of your life on the motorway, with most of your sustenance coming from service stations. Every professional musician will have a favourite service station. You end up knowing them like landmarks on a map. In the UK, my personal favourite is Beaconsfield but Oxford Services is a close runner-up, being home to The Secret Burrito (touring British musician in-joke). You can even do your laundry in Cobham Services. But it's very difficult to eat consistently and healthily on the motorway. Eating McDonalds at 3am can leave you tired and grumpy because you're not putting good energy into your body. And if you have to get up and do it all again the following day it's a killer, especially if you have to stay awake on the death drive home with only a Ginsters pasty and a Monster energy drink to fuel you. This is why so many musicians burn out in their late twenties. They've had enough of cold pasties at 3am and getting home to their partner shouting at them. This is also why a lot of bigger bands will budget for a personal trainer. Reuben, my personal trainer, goes on tour with Royal Blood a lot. They pay him to keep them in shape. There's a lot of money riding on the bigger bands and a lot of pressure to not fuck up. How would you feel about letting down 20,000 of your fans, who have travelled to see you perform?

But it's just as important for smaller bands too. When you're starting out you can't afford to get ill and lose gigs. Especially now that one of the only sources of real money for musicians is from gigs. I've done gigs with sick band members puking into a bucket backstage because we couldn't afford to not go on. You have to get through in whatever way you can. You have a responsibility to your bandmates and audience to stay healthy.

It really is possible to eat healthily on the road. Most service stations in the UK will have an M&S outlet, which is great for healthy food. Or you could prepare food to bring with you, or allow yourself enough time to get off the motorway and go and get some proper food.

Of course, staying healthy on the road isn't just about food. If you're shifting your own gear as well as performing you'll be doing a lot of exercise. Be careful not to pull muscles when shifting gear at 3am.

Touring is a life of excess and I'm not just talking drink and drugs here. Everything happens to excess, including procrastination, boredom and travelling. This can make it very easy to look elsewhere for recreation and sustenance, in drugs, alcohol, gambling, prostitution and drinking. A lot of musicians buy into the myth of sex, drugs and rock 'n' roll but this lifestyle only ever brings short term gain.

The best musicians I know are machines; they're indestructible. It's a mentality thing. Luke, the guitarist in The Indie Killers, sets out for every gig with an entire carrier bag of pharmaceuticals that get rid of just about every possible ailment. He once did a gig with pneumonia. Our drummer once did a gig with a broken foot. As I said before, if gigging is your band's only source of income, the show must go on. You literally cannot afford to let your bandmates down.

How not to kill your band mates

Every band starts out as best mates and it's a total love-in and you want to spend every waking hour together. Then you go on tour together for a year and the dynamic changes. The main reason life on the road can make you want to kill your bandmates is because it's a bit like being in prison. There's nowhere to escape to. If you're touring in a van or minibus you will only be a maximum of two or three feet away from your bandmates at all times. Then, when you get out of the van and go into the venue, you're still the same distance away, only this time you're on a stage. Then it's back in the van again, or if you're staying overnight in a hotel, chances are you'll be sharing a room and, very worst case scenario if you're on a tight budget, a bed. It's like you're shackled to your bandmates at all times. Let's face it, even the best friendship in the world would be tested by this.

When you spend so much time together it's easy to run out of things to say to each other. You can't ask each other how your day went because you know only too well, you've been with them 24/7. You quickly run out of small talk and pleasantries and it's enough to drive you stir crazy. Over a long period of time the tiniest thing can drive you to want to murder, from what socks they wear, to the way they pronounce a certain word, or even the way they breathe!

It's totally irrational how much these things can affect you, they might seem trivial with hindsight but in the moment it's like someone's punched your mum. It's a cauldron where everything is amplified by ten. So, what can you do about this? How can you alleviate the tension? Here are my suggestions...

Avoid hot topics

Certain subjects should be out of bounds. I know football brings a lot of people together but some musicians hate it with a passion. If this is the case, just leave it. Try and find common ground that won't annoy people. Similarly, politics is a big no no, unless you're all on exactly the same page. It's just not worth it. The last thing you want to do is have a massive ruck about whether Donald Trump should build a wall and then have to go on stage.

Bring earplugs

Always take earplugs on tour – the squidgy variety – because the chances are someone in your band will snore and the chances are, they're the one you'll have to share a hotel room with. I've lost count of the amount of times I've seriously contemplated taking a life sentence in prison in exchange for smothering someone at 2am in a Travelodge so I can get some sleep. One night on tour I woke up needing the toilet and the guitarist was snoring away in the bed next to mine. I walked into the bathroom feeling dazed and groggy and started going to the toilet. Then I heard someone clearing his throat to the left of me. The drummer was wrapped up in a duvet in the bath with his head only about two foot away from my dick. He was there because he couldn't sleep because of the earth shattering snoring. Moral of the story: always bring earplugs.

Help don't hinder

The biggest thing to remember is that you're trying to help your bandmates as opposed to getting on their nerves. You need to be self-aware and ask 'how can I make their lives easier?' If someone in your band is making things harder you need to have a chat about it to sort it out. Have regular air-clearers within the band to check everyone's OK. This can be a great way of diffusing the pressure. Also, make sure to take some time away from each other between touring.

How to maximise time on the road

One thing nobody tells you about life on the road is how much time you have. Not only when you're en route to the venue but once you get there too. Waiting for set-up and sound check could take up to one or two hours. Then, once the sound check is done, you have even more time to wait before the show. And then you have the journey home.

> *The great thing about all of this spare time is that it provides you with a real opportunity to build your long-term career.*

You could use it for content creation, marketing, networking and building a website. However, despite the best intentions, most musicians aren't that proactive with their spare time. It's worth flagging up an uncomfortable truth here; the band you're in could come to an end at any moment, so it's really important to use the spare time you get to build your own foundation. You need to be prepared for every eventuality. Don't make the same mistake as a lot of musicians and live for the day. You need to plan for tomorrow too. You could use your spare time on the road to build some kind of passive income, such as selling things on Shopify or Amazon FBA or investing in stocks and shares. It doesn't have to be music-related. You could also use the time to improve on your playing. And you could be networking and messaging and updating your socials. You could even learn a new language!

When you're 25 you feel as if you're going to be young forever. Then, all of a sudden, you're 40. What if you don't want to do it anymore? What if you can't do it anymore? You need to be prepared for the inevitable changes that are going to happen. I get that this can be hard, especially if, at every opportunity, your bandmates are hollering 'let's go to the pub!' I dread to think how many hours/days/weeks/months I've wasted hanging round in pubs while I've been on the road. It's about getting the balance right. You need to get on well with your bandmates but equally you need to build your foundation. Hopefully, once your bandmates see what you're doing, they'll be inspired to maximise their spare time too. You could even do something proactive together as a team.

Don't just create memories, document them

This section is a bit of a crossover from my first book, *The Rule-Breaker's Guide to Social Media*, where I talked about how bands can take control of their careers by building and looking after an audience. The great thing about the recent changes to the music industry is that there's no middle man any more. The barriers that used to scupper so many musicians' entry into the industry have gone. However, building an audience is time consuming. One of the best ways to do this is via your social media channels.

In my opinion, being on the road is the best time to create social media content. You've got the romance and excitement of being on tour, which people really want to see, the band are all together and you're going to different places *and*, as established in the previous section, you've got time to document the story of being on tour and show the world who you are and what you do. The trouble is, so many bands forget to document what they're doing. Great things are happening but it's not being captured and it's such a lost opportunity. Forgetfulness is unacceptable at this stage. If it helps, make someone responsible for documenting your life on the road. Make it a part of the show. At the time of writing this book, the easiest way of documenting what you're doing on the road is on Instagram, especially using Insta Stories. If you post videos and photos there they can automatically be shared to other platforms too.

Many years ago, I was at a Jason Mraz gig and at the end of the night during the final song, Jason pulled out an old Polaroid camera, balanced it on the bass amp and the band posed for a shot with the crowd in the background. While the picture developed Mraz finished the song, waving it to dry it, then thanked the audience and made his way off the stage clutching his photo. I imagined him having an awesome photo album full of Polaroids, telling the story of a thousand gigs. The next night, I was on a gig with the boys and towards the end, I told the crowd to squash in and we took a photo together. When we finished I uploaded the pic to our Facebook page and people who'd been at the gig started tagging themselves and sharing it. The next day I had two separate enquiries about the band from people who'd seen the picture. They'd seen the crowd having fun in the photo and it made them want to book us, so that they and their friends and family could enjoy a similar experience.

The best thing about this is it's so easy. All you have to do is turn on the camera on your phone. Discuss what you want to achieve from your socials early in the day of a gig or even before the tour starts. It can really help to plan this stuff in advance, as well as capturing all the great spontaneous moments. You could start with some content about where you're going tonight. Then have something from you and the band while you're en route and arriving at the venue. Then you could document a little bit of the sound check and the crowd before you go on. At the end of the gig, get a shot or a video of the crowd singing a song. After the gig, you could take pictures of fans and tag them and finish with a post thanking everyone for coming. In short, it really pays to plan!

Friday drive day

One of the best pieces of advice I can give to any musician travelling on a Friday is ALLOW EXTRA TIME! However long you think it's going to take you to get to your venue, add at least three hours. I'm not joking. Whatever your sat nav says, double it. The reason for this is that on Fridays everyone and his or her auntie is going somewhere and the roads are chock-a-block. At the end of the day, it's far better to be three hours early than three hours late (see earlier section on maximising your spare time).

Being late is horrible. The venue and other bands on the bill will be pissed off. You won't have the time to sound check properly, you're going to go in feeling unprepared. And, if one day will catch you out more than any other, it's Friday. Whenever we have a gig on a Friday we clear the diary and get to the venue silly early and use any extra time to be proactive. Respect Friday drive day!

Dealing with sound limiters

As an accomplished musician you will play in many different types of venues throughout your career – usually throughout any given month – and they will all have different sound implications. It would be completely impractical to take five different versions of your instrument or types of gear to cover all possible eventualities, so you end up with a one size fits all set up. Nowadays, with the population getting bigger and areas becoming more built up, venues are increasingly under pressure to keep on top of noise complaints and many of them have been forced to have a sound limiter fitted by the council.

A sound limiter is a box connected to a wall with a mic attached and it measures the decibels of the music playing. When it hits a certain decibel over a certain period of time the limiter will cut the power to the stage. The scary thing about this is that every venue with a sound limiter will have a different sound or frequency problem for you to deal with. You might be playing a limiter that's set to 90 decibels but it's 30 feet in front of you, so you can get away with it. On the other hand, a limiter might be set to 98 decibels but it's positioned right behind the drum-kit, or you're playing in a stone or glass-walled room, which amplifies the sound. Basically, you're not just fighting the limiter, you're fighting the room.

A couple of years ago, I did 18 stadium gigs in a year as a contract for Sky TV, playing at half time during football matches. As soon as the players ran off we'd have to run on and play for ten minutes. We were playing on a stage in the middle of the pitch, which meant that the slap-back from the stadium was huge because of the dome shape. This meant we had to play at bedroom volumes for them to amplify it to the stadium. It was so weird because, playing in a stadium, your instinct is to crash it up to the maximum volume, but when it's set up for a football match it's like playing in your bedroom with your mum downstairs! So, how do we tackle these frustrating limiter gigs?

Firstly, you have to tackle the sound of the drum kit. I would always recommend a drummer carry plastic rods not bamboo, as they're made up of thin strings of plastic with lots of air in between, so it stops the noise level. Also, bamboo rods break far too easily when you play a rock gig. Plastic won't break and it's quieter. Always carry gaffer tape too. Taping the drums deadens the drum-kit. It might sound terrible but it's better than the sound being cut. Sometime you have to take extreme measures just to get through the gig. In really extreme cases I'd put a tea-towel over the snare drum. It enables you to get the power and the energy without the heavy hitting sound.

I'd have an alternative go-to set-up for other instruments too. As a bass player, I use valve amps (2 x Orange AD200 Head's to be precise) and Fender Precision basses. If there is a limiter I'd probably use a jazz bass or even an active bass and a solid state amp, just to get more control over the frequencies and, while this leads to a miserable gig where I sound like I'm playing through cardboard boxes, needs must!

Guitars don't usually affect limiters as much as the bass does so you can get away with more. The key with guitars isn't the frequency, it's making sure you're not overpowering the vocals. If you make the vocalist have to sing louder it will set off the limiter. Things like having a single coil guitar can help and even, dare I say it, a guitar pod (I know, I know, it's far from ideal). With an amp you're moving and pushing air, with a pod you have a lot more control over the frequencies because you're processing the sound going straight into the PA. Please don't get me wrong, for anyone who takes their sound seriously these are all horrible things to have to do, but sometimes you have to do what's needed to get through a gig and live to play another day. I know limiters are a pain in the arse but the fact is, if they were taken away they'd have to close down half the venues that allow musicians to make a living.

The gods of the gigs – the music industry's dark secret

Anyone who gigs on a weekly basis will know of these gig gods, although some of you might refer to them as "sods law" or "just my luck". But I prefer to think of them as a group of gods with a very warped sense of humour, who control all aspects of our gigging life. So, how do you know when these supreme beings are interfering with your life on the road? Here are some of the tell-tale signs to look out for...

1. No matter where you are playing in the country, you will not arrive home before 2am. Even if you are playing a local gig and finish at 11pm, something random will happen to delay you and ensure you don't walk in your front door before 2.

2. If you only take one guitar to a gig, you will break more strings than you ever have before in your life. They will be flying off your axe like toenail clippings at a pedicure shop. However, if you take a spare guitar, your strings will become stronger than Thor!

3. If you leave for your gig with hours to spare, the roads will be clear and you will arrive with more time than you started with. However, if you leave with no spare time, prepare for every road to be full of caravans, accidents and new roadworks.

4. Eating before a gig will ensure that your client provides you with a large meal, leaving you stuffed and feeling sick immediately prior to performing. If you fail to eat beforehand however, you'll discover that your gig is in the middle of nowhere, your client has no food and you'll only have car mints and a lip salve for sustenance.

I first wrote about these signs in the van on the way to the first of three gigs. By the time I got to this point we'd been stopped by the police, weighed and fined for being overweight. Over the next three days, I blew a bass cab, got stuck in three hours of traffic, had one of the worst gigs in the band's history and to top it all, on the way back home, we ran over a cat at 60mph. As far as I'm concerned, this is irrefutable proof that the gods of the gigs are very real and don't like the attention. They are like the MI5, the mafia or the new Metallica album; you know they exist, but it's better to pretend that they don't. Be warned!

Hygiene

Because of the way you travel in bands, i.e. closer than you probably would with your friends and family, you need to make sure you're not inflicting any unpleasant hygiene issues on your fellow band members. Let's face it, musicians can be smelly bastards. They can be lazy too. If it comes down to a choice between a shower in the morning or an extra ten minutes in the hotel bed the bed's usually the winner. But then everyone else has to pay the price. If hygiene is an issue in your band forget about diplomacy. Tell the culprit they need to take a shower. It's far better to clear the air, excuse the pun, than start festering away with resentment.

Clean clothes are important too. Make sure you don't sling your sweaty stuff from the night before on top of your clean stuff in your bag. And make sure you pack enough clothes for regular changes. Touring is a very sweaty environment. You get stinky quite quick on the road and if you don't have clean clothes to change into the next day, any benefits of a shower will fade pretty quick.

No pooping on the tour bus

Tour buses nowadays are incredible. They're like houses on wheels, they're like some incredible episode of *Amazing Spaces*, where they've made something the size of a small living room look like a spaceship. But there's one slight problem – you're never more than 12 feet away from the toilet. The first time I went on a tour bus there was a sign on the toilet door saying, '**NO POOPING ON THE TOUR BUS!**' I asked what happened if someone needed to go and I was told that they'd stop at the services. With eight of us on the bus I didn't really see how this was practical, wouldn't we be stopping all the time?! But I was told that this was no problem because anything was better than someone going on the bus, which was basically like someone shitting in the living room. It's amazing how a band are able to synchronise their bowel movements. I always find it really funny that there's this unwritten – or sometimes even written – rule that there should be no pooping. The fact is, as stated before, musicians don't tend to have the healthiest diet. Six pints of Stella plus a dodgy burger is not going to have the happiest outcome.

Relationship sacrifices

Being on the road can really take its toll on relationships. You're either at home with your partner loads or away for long periods of time. There's no happy medium. Even in a covers band you're away three or four times a week. And while you're away, you'll be out having fun and enjoying yourself, which can make even the most confident partner feel insecure. The brutal truth is, it can be very difficult to be busy touring and maintain a relationship. I know this all too well, personally. My ex used to frequently call herself a "band widow".

It's also very difficult to take holidays as a musician, because your busiest times are seasonal i.e. summer and Christmas. Since I started gigging at 17 there have only been two years when I haven't played a New Tear's Eve gig. And one of them was only down to a last minute cancellation by the venue during the stresses of the Millennium Bug predictions of 1999-2000! Other special occasions often get sacrificed to gigging too, such as your partner's birthday or Valentine's Day. No partner wants to be left alone on those days but if your band have to cancel gigs because of your personal life, you could be hampering their careers and your success. The painful truth is, you have to make sacrifices if you want to do well. The trouble is, the more you play, the better you'll get and the more gigs you'll be offered. And if you want to pay the bills, you have to say yes to them.

All of the relationships I was in while I was a gigging musician ended because I was in a band, so I'm painfully aware that I'm the not the best person to give advice on this subject. One thing I would say is that communication is key, and the more you communicate with your partner, the better.

Part Six: Gear

Like most musicians, I am a gear geek. I'm also incredibly judgemental of gear, especially other people's. But I do understand that gear is designed to do different jobs and it depends on what musicians are prioritising. For example, the size and the weight versus the sound, or what musical genre they're in. However, whilst there is some subjectivity, there's also what's known in the trade as "industry standard gear" – not to be confused with what I would class as "music shop gear". This chapter is designed around the priorities of a musician, with regards to budget, time, and gear etiquette.

Gear does not maketh a god

In all the years I was teaching in music colleges I was most heavily linked to the bass department, which means that I've taught thousands of bass classes. The amount of money that some of my students would spend on gear was preposterous. I always found it inspirational when I saw people saving for years to buy the guitar they wanted, but you can get to a point where you're prioritising your gear over your career.

An example of this was when I taught an evening class for people who couldn't do full-time courses. It was in quite a posh part of Surrey, so I think it's fair to say that most of them had a lot of disposable income. One of them even owned a helicopter. Guitars were their passion and practically every week someone would turn up with a new instrument they'd spent thousands on. Some of their guitars more expensive than my car. OK, so my car wasn't exactly worth a fortune but that's not the point! However, there was one key problem – they'd spend a load of money on a guitar but they hardly ever practised. They seemed to think that by buying the same guitar as Eric Clapton, it would make them play like Eric Clapton but of course it meant nothing.

> *Their sound didn't get any better because that had to come from their fingers and their authority.*

They didn't put nearly enough time into their technique and learning. They wanted to bypass all of that. Us teachers were so envious of their guitars but the irony is, we had what really counted – we could play.

Gear is very important, in that it needs to work and you need to sound professional, but you must never lose sight of the fact that your music comes from you and your personality. Usually, an emotional person will show their emotions in their playing, ditto an authoritative person. The power, the sound, the tone and the groove comes mostly from you. You could give John Mayer ten different guitars and he'd sound like him on every one of them. His personality comes out whenever he plays, it's all in his unique technique and feel.

As previously stated in this book, being a musician and trying to have a long-term career is not only difficult but quite expensive. You need money for promotion and image and marketing and if you can't afford to do those things but you're looking across your bedroom at a two grand guitar I put it to you that you might need to change your priorities.

A couple of years ago I bought a Fender jazz bass copy. It wasn't even a known brand, it was something someone had made from bits. The musical equivalent of someone taking a Vauxhall Nova and trying to make it look like a Mercedes sports car. I bought it for £120 and it will be absolutely fine for me to use as my working bass for the next twenty years. It's got a good sound and does everything I need it to. I also have an eighties Jaydee Supernatural bass, a la Mark King, which is luminous pink and probably worth several thousand pounds. While it's a beautiful ornament, it would never work as my professional bass in a million years. It's all about having the right gear to do the job, putting time, effort and money into practise and building your career, rather than investing everything in that new mega chorus delay flange loop pedal!

The festival set up

I've called this section the festival set up but it also applies to most support slots, in other words, when you're not headlining at a gig and have limited time to act up. When this is the case it's important to realise that the sound crew are not there to look after you. In fact, you're generally a thorn in their side because they have other acts to look after and you're not the priority. Therefore, your job is to get the best sound you can as quickly as possible so everyone working in the crew at that festival isn't remembering you for the wrong reasons.

This is where the gear you choose becomes critical. I see so many guitarists with the biggest pedal boards ever or even worse, one of those multi-effects units, which always has a power cable that looks as if it's made of paper and could break at any moment. As soon as you plug all of this stuff in and it doesn't work, panic sets in. Is it a battery or a cable or a power lead that's faulty? You have no immediate way of knowing and you've only got five minutes to sound check and get off again. I'd always recommend making your gear set up as simple and quick as possible. As a bass player I always have a valve amp, usually my two orange AD200 bass amp heads into two ampeg cabs. My pedal-board is so minimal. I have a tuner, an EQ pedal and an octave pedal to boost in some lows. It means I can set up my entire rig in one minute flat.

This also taps into what I was saying earlier in this book about making yourself irreplaceable.

Being good to go in just one or two minutes makes everyone else happy with me, which in turn, makes me more employable.

When it comes to festivals I tend to recommend the five minute rule. Usually when you're not headlining, you get a line check not a sound check, which is basically the minimum they can get away with. They'll probably check the guitar and bass are coming out front and go through the drums to make sure the mics are working. If you're lucky you might get thirty seconds to run a bit of a song but this is only if you're lucky. The festival will be running all day. You just turn up for your slot, set up your bits and hit a few notes to make sure it works. The sound crew will do everything else on the fly once you've started playing. Usually, there will be an out front sound guy and an on stage sound guy.

Going out on stage to play to an audience when you have no idea what it's going to sound like is terrifying. You have no idea if the guitar next to you is going to deafen you or if you'll even hear the hi-hat for the drums or the vocals. And this isn't a case of *what if*, this is a case of *what happens*. I'm sure it's probably happened to you at some point. You've gone on stage all fired up to play, the audience are watching, excited. You turn everything on. You play something, a note, and you realise that there's nothing. At this point, your bum-hole turns into a flappy paddle gear box. Every second that passes feels like an eternity and it's your fault. You're looking down at the light on the pedal board, thinking, *what do I do*? Don't get me wrong, sound guys are great and they will be able to fix it but there will always be a few seconds while they're fixing it where you'll be shitting yourself. At least if you know that it's probably going to happen you can be prepared. In summary, until you are alongside the likes of Muse headlining, bringing too much gear will make yours and other people's lives harder. On festival stages, less is most definitely more.

Take pride in your gear

I've spent the last ten years auditioning musicians for my music management company, DK Management. We have a simple live audition process and we hold auditions all over the country. We have auditioned, guitar, bass, drum, string and brass players and vocalists, and some of the gear they turn up with never ceases to amaze me. An audition is like a job interview. You will be judged partly on your personality but mostly on your playing and professionalism. If someone doesn't turn up with the right gear how can they possibly expect to be taken seriously as a professional? I've seen a whole array of 'gear crimes' in my time auditioning, but the most common offences are turning up with amps or pedals that crackle, drumsticks that look as if they've been chewed to death by a dog, broken guitar strings and separate pedals which aren't in pedal boards. Turning up with no lead is another common one. How are do you expect to play without a lead? Mime playing, while singing your part down the mic?!

I read a study last week on a statistical website which estimates that there are 50,000 working musicians in the UK, but that figure includes every aspect of the music industry, from teaching, covers bands and sessioning, right through to the likes of Ed Sheeran. Every year, there are 50,000 more wannabe musicians in the music education system. That's effectively 50,000 more people graduating every year looking for jobs. And that doesn't include people not in the education system. This means there's a huge supply and demand issue. If you want to break through you need to do everything you can to be better than everyone else. One area where you can have an easy win over other musicians is turning up with the right working gear. It's amazing how many people don't do this. If we audition fifteen people it's likely that six or seven of them won't be in with a chance because we took one look at their gear and realised they wouldn't be able to do the gig. That's one third to a half of all auditionees losing out because we've judged their professionalism before they've even played. That's the harsh reality of the world we live in. But you can do yourself a favour and make sure you're in the group that doesn't fall at the first hurdle.

The stories behind your gear

If you think about it, quite a lot of musical heroes feature their instrument in their story. Everyone knows that BB King's guitar is named Lucille and Noel Gallagher's Union Jack Epiphone became instantly recognisable. In the world of social media where everyone's watching, you can definitely use your gear to your advantage. Whether you feature your gear as part of a great story or in building your brand, there are many benefits to becoming synonymous with an instrument.

A really great story behind an instrument can also help when it comes to being interviewed. I used to co-host a radio show and part of my job was to interview young bands. The problem was, because they were just starting out, they didn't have many stories. One thing that we could talk about though was their gear. Gear is a great leveller, something all musicians can talk about, regardless of experience, or lack of. The same applies in auditions. Having a good story about your gear is a great ice-breaker when meeting new people.

I have one bass that I call *my* bass – it's what I would use whenever I do a photoshoot or professional gig. It's the bass I use for my brand. I have other guitars, which do different jobs, but that's the one I want to be seen with. Now let me tell you the story behind it...

When I was a kid the first concert I ever went to was when my dad took me to see The Stranglers. I was only about fourteen at the time and didn't know much about music but the bass player – the great JJ Burnell – had a black P Bass and I thought it was coolest thing I'd ever seen. As soon as I started playing professionally I knew that I had to get a P Bass too because it had made such an impact on me. I found one and fell in love with it and that's been my go-to bass ever since. My current P Bass is absolutely battered, it looks like it's been attached to a car and driven down the street. It's also the heaviest bass I own but it's the bass for me. When it all went wrong with BIMM and I didn't know what to do or who to turn to, the first thing I did was pick up that bass because it felt like a family member to me. Playing it gave me comfort and strength in my time of need.

Have a think about your favourite instrument and why you chose it. Maybe it was passed down to you, or maybe it's home-made, or maybe it's travelled the world with you. How did you feel when you first played it? What is the finest moment you had with that instrument? Has it had any near misses? Maybe you couldn't care less about your gear – that's a story in itself.

At the end of the day, instruments are beautiful things and they're full of stories that inspire emotion. Every time you play your instrument you're potentially creating another story. And if you're ever stuck for something to post on social media, try posting a photo of your instrument with the caption, *I remember this one time when...* Fill in the dots and you're away.

Spare gear

As discussed in the earlier section on gigs, when playing live, things can and do go wrong. What my 2,000 plus gigs have taught me is to be prepared and ready for the unexpected. I try to make sure that I'm able to get through any gig whatever happens. This means I take two instruments. Not because I need them but because I don't want to be the guy holding things up because I've snapped a string. In my band we carry spare amps and spare equipment but we don't carry two of everything. It's not realistic to do that. You know that weird runt of a spare wheel you get in a car, the one that looks more like a bike wheel and you can't go over 50 mph on it but it will get you home? I'd say the same applies for gear. I carry any spares I can fit in but if I'm carrying a massive valve amp, it's not feasible to carry two or three of them however, I can have a little pocket-sized pedal or head if I need a replacement to get me through the gig. Usually they don't sound all that great but sometimes you just have to get through the gig. Spare leads, batteries, drumsticks and drumheads all enable you to get the job done.

This isn't just important from an equipment and audience point of view, it's a career choice.

> *Being a musician is so much about building momentum.*

If you're not able to fulfil a contract you'll get complaints and bad feedback, and nothing stops a band's momentum faster than bad feedback. This is about making sure that those wheels keep rolling and don't slow down. Trying to get back up to speed once you've stopped is very difficult.

We used to have a live performance class at BIMM that only took place once in the three years a student was there. It was called the "What if it Breaks" class. We'd deliberately set up a rehearsal with wonky leads and broken strings. It wasn't just about the students getting through the gig it was about keeping the energy and momentum of the gig going. It was a test of how quickly they were able to respond and change things.

Another thing to note here is the importance of having your spares on you. What's the point in having a spare bass drum pedal if you keep it in the van and have to stop the gig to go out and get it? You need to know where everything is and be able to quickly access it.

Using other bands' gear

Often, if there are a number of bands on a bill, there will be some kind of gear share. This helps avoid the inconvenience of having to take everything off in between sets and makes the sound check much easier, but it can have its pitfalls too. You need to respect another musician's gear, especially if you're a guitarist, as they tend to be precious about their amp and sound. Drummers on the other hand don't tend to give a shit. The drumming community is incredible – always there to have a laugh and help each other. If you are using someone else's drum kit however, it's good to bring your own breakables, such as cymbals, snare and bass drum pedals. The rest of the kit can stay intact on stage mic-ed up.

It might seem like common sense to respect another person's gear but I think we probably all have horror stories about our gear being badly treated. Singers swinging mics around, big tub-thumping drummers beating the shit out of your drum kit, or guitarists and bass players placing their pint on your

amp, which is always going to go wrong. While it seems obvious, it's an ongo-
ing occurrence. I remember watching a band who were doing a gear share and
when it got to end of their show they did the classic Nirvana-style routine of
smashing things up. This is fine when it's your gear, but in this case it was the
venue's. Not only were the band banned from that venue but word got out via
social media and several of the other gigs on their tour got pulled. They ended
up getting banned from all the venues in their area and had to split up because
they couldn't get gigs. All because they treated someone else's gear like it was
their own. If you don't embrace the community and have respect for the people you meet, you'll struggle to get gigs long term.

Part Seven: Marketing

The first thing we need to do in this section is acknowledge the elephant in the room, which is that the music industry is a fashion-based industry and talent will only take you so far. After a while, how you look and how you promote yourself becomes just as important as your playing. When you have thousands of students leaving music college every year all trying to break into the same sphere you need to be able to cut through the noise, you need to be able to market yourself in a way that is powerful and memorable. Of all the chapters in this book this is the one that will help you the most when it comes to setting yourself apart from the competition.

Photos

Photos are the natural starting point in this chapter because a photo really does say a thousand words. So often in this industry a photo is the first impression you get of a musician and you can tell a lot about them from it. You can tell if they're fashionable. You can tell if they've got high standards. You can tell what gear they use. I've spent the last ten years training musicians in how to get work and a key thing I advise is to have regular photo shoots – and to take photo shoots seriously. I can't believe how many shoots I've seen where musicians haven't made any effort whatsoever. They haven't coordinated their clothes, they haven't bothered getting a haircut, they're sporting fungus beards, they haven't ironed their clothes – and they're usually the wrong size clothes. It doesn't matter how good the photographer is, it's impossible to make someone who looks like a scruffy student look like a rock star, but it's easy to make a rock star look amazing.

One of the first things any band should do is look at the quality of pictures that run through their marketing. Back in the day, a band would set up one shoot and be able to use the shots in all of their marketing but nowadays, because of social media, bands need to be appearing in photos on a weekly basis. This is something you need to be prepared for. You need to be prepared for people sticking their phones in your face at gigs. You need to be prepared to take photos of your rehearsals and behind the scenes at a gig. You need to represent yourself as a musician at all times.

> *The days of looking like a band on-stage and scruffy off-stage are gone. Now you need to look like a musician at all times.*

It's very important to set up regular professional photo shoots. DIY photo shoots only work if you have someone around you with a very keen eye, someone who understands lighting, angles and shots. A really good photo shoot with a photographer who knows what they're doing will make the band feel at ease and capture the best pictures. I'd recommend that you have a photo shoot once a month at least because of the never-ending need for content. In marketing terms, a really amazing photo could be the difference between you getting your foot in the door for a gig, or on the front page of a magazine, or being asked to an audition. Great photos bring your social media to life too. In short, they make you look cool.

Tips for a photo shoot

A good photo shoot is all about the pre-planning; the more time you spend preparing for it, the better it will be. Here are some tips to help you get the most from your photo shoots...

- Pick a location and understand what would work best in that location i.e. what to wear and whether to use instruments
- Co-ordinate what you are going to wear to create an overall band look
- Book haircuts and beard trims for a day or two before
- Make sure you've got time to set the shot up beforehand
- Make sure that the photographer knows what you're trying to achieve in advance so they know what gear to bring down and how to light the shoot. Let them know if it's going to be in a dark room
- Make sure your clothes aren't creased or dirty – unless of course that's the look you're after!

Videos

The only thing that might work better than a professional photo in marketing terms is a video. Videos are the best way of showing off who you are and what you can do. If you're looking for work as a session musician spend some time learning video production and then post videos of you playing on your social media every week. This will really help to set you apart from most other musicians because the sad truth is a lot of musicians are inconsistent and lazy. There might be hundreds of thousands of musicians out there looking for work but when you narrow that down to how many of them are capable and professional, this number rapidly diminishes.

This is actually great news because, if you are willing to go that extra mile with your marketing, there's not a lot of competition at all.

It's the equivalent of comparing how many people have a car and can drive to how many could hack it on a race track. Use this fact to inspire rather than intimidate you and see it as your job to get into that minority through things like professional videos of your playing.

It's so important to think about the bigger picture. If you're trying to get auditions, the fact that you can play is great but do you also look good and confident enough to fit in on that stage? If I was trying to get gigs I'd be making videos of me playing pieces of music that are interesting and complex so that I could show off my skills, and I'd be making these videos on a weekly basis. Think creatively. Are there any tracks that you could put your own unique twist on? You could try playing along to a loop rather than a full track. Stop assuming that people will know who you are and what you're about. Show them why you're better than the competition. Show how you're stretching yourself and learning in your videos.

The great thing is, it's so simple to set up your camera and record yourself and so easy to share those videos on all of the main social media platforms, such as Instagram, Facebook and YouTube. And you can use the YouTube link to send the video to people. Sharing a video is a great way to start networking and conversations.

When it comes to quality the same rule applies to videos as to photos. If you're not prepared to learn how to make a good video you're going to be letting your playing down. Find out about things like lighting and angles, put some thought into where to shoot it. It all comes down to attention to detail. Before you post a video online or send it anywhere ask, *does it look good, sound good, and is the background good?* Would you be happy to send the video to a record label for an audition? It's human instinct to want to take shortcuts but if you want to succeed you have to pay attention to everything.

Networking

I don't think anyone likes networking, myself included. I hate networking events. I find them really cheesy and awkward. I'd much rather play for someone or have someone come to me. But at least now there's digital networking, which is a lot easier than networking in the flesh and you can pretty much get hold of anyone online. You can even tweet the American President and tell him what you think of him! And now, rather than just having a business card to hand out to people, you've got a plethora of online content to back you up – or you should have.

Every day I receive about 100 messages on social media from musicians. They introduce themselves and send me a link to their stuff. I'm always really shocked by the number of people who show me content that's either unfinished or in such a state they have to makes excuses or apologies for it. About 50% of the time people will apologise for certain aspects of their marketing when they're trying to network with me. I don't understand why they don't just fix these things before they reach out to me. It's like going to a meeting and apologising for not showering for three days. Why not just have a shower first rather than showing up stinky? The whole point of networking is to try and build relationships that will help you in your career. You want to introduce yourself in the best way possible and create the right impression, so make sure your house is in order.

I probably recruit about 50 people a year across my various businesses. I could be hiring a musician or a PA or a videographer or a sales person, but whatever role I'm recruiting for, the first thing I'll do when I get sent a CV is take a look at the candidate's social media. I'm always surprised by the embarrassing things people have on their socials, which I assume they wouldn't want a future employer to see. Before you reach out to someone for networking reasons have a quick check of your social media platforms and make sure you're happy with everything that's out there about you.

To recap, here are the three steps you need to take when it comes to networking...

1. *Get your house in order before approaching anyone*
2. *Allocate time to network on a weekly basis*
3. *Get clear on what value you'll be giving the person you want to network with, as well as what you want from them*

Regarding this last point, I'd love to be able to chat to legendary entrepreneur and internet personality Gary Vaynerchuk, but why would he want to talk to me? If I could find something of value to offer him then maybe he would, so I'd need to get clear on that before I think about what he could do for me. Networking isn't just about what's in it for you but what's in it for them too. It has to be a two-way deal.

How you're contactable

How you're contactable is crucial – and more complicated than it's ever been. This is because there are now so many ways to contact people, and everyone has their preferred way. Some people use Instagram messages as if they're email. Others are strictly Facebook messenger. And others prefer to contact people via Twitter or LinkedIn. There are so many ways people can get in touch with you it can be easy to miss communications. Therefore, it's very important to make it clear how you want to be contacted on your social media or website, with clear calls to action, such as, *'for bookings please email this address'*.

Having said all this, it's important to be flexible and open to other people's preferred way of messaging. The last thing you want to do is miss out on a gig because you have a phobia of WhatsApp. Make sure you're contactable across all the different platforms and make sure you regularly check your messages.

Another crucial element when it comes to being contactable is how professional and punctual you are at replying. I need to make it clear that I'm not an expert when it comes to organisation so this subject is definitely not my speciality but on the platforms where I want to be able to communicate instantly and reply on a minute by minute basis, I always set up notifications on my phone. I turn my notifications off on other platforms so I'm not getting bombarded and I'll set aside time in the evening to go through the comments and messages. You can have some control over your communications and you don't have to have everything pinging at you all the time. You get to decide your priorities.

Make sure you allocate some time every day to go through all of your messages. If you aren't able to reply to them all in one go, prioritise. Reply straight away to the ones that can't be left, and leave the others until an easier time. I try not to leave it longer than 24 hours before getting back to anyone, otherwise it starts verging on unprofessional.

Another really important tip when it comes to communications is to make sure you have a professional email address. *hornypixie_67@hotmail.com* might have been a great option back when you were 15, but maybe it's not giving off quite the right impression now you're trying to be taken seriously as a musician. There are so many different email providers you can easily get a professional-sounding address.

Merchandise

As already established, due to the likes of YouTube and Spotify effectively giving away music for free it's become essential for bands to find other ways of making money. Selling merch is a great way to do this. When I was in The Indie Killers we whacked our tracks on to a CD and had a thousand printed to take with us to our gigs. We let people know there were CDs available via banners at the side of stage. After six months of gigs they'd all gone and we'd made £8,000 profit. This was great because it was completely passive income. And not only was it a way of making money, but it was a great marketing tool too because everyone who bought a CD would be way more likely to remember us the next time they were looking for a band for a party. We got guitar picks printed with our details on for similar reasons.

> *Merch can be such a great way for musicians to build and market their brand.*

If people enjoy your gig they'll want a memento for nostalgia reasons. Your job is to tap into that need at different price points. Don't just think CDs and t-shirts, have smaller things for people who might not have much money, like picks, wrist-bands, stickers and pin badges.

A note of caution here: if you see merch as simply a way of making a quick buck rather than providing value for your audience you won't get away with it for long. The quality of the merch is reflective of your brand. So, if your t-shirt is cut badly and feels cheap, it's going to create a similar impression about your band and music. I'd recommend you use a professional to design you an image. You can use the same image across all of your merch to keep the costs down.

Another tip is to try and keep some merch on you at all times, as you never know when a marketing opportunity might present itself. Have merch available for sale on your website too. And it's well worth having a payment facility on your phone so you're able to sell anywhere. Giving a couple of t-shirts away during a gig can be a great way of selling them too, as it draws the crowd's attention to them.

The power of sold out

Being sold out is one of the most powerful marketing tools in the business as it shows you're in high demand. In order to create this perception you need to limit the number of things you're selling. This works well with everything. For instance, if you make a print run of 50 CDs and you sell out within a day and people are still emailing for copies, chances are they'll tell other people about their disappointment at not getting one and effectively do your marketing for you. The same goes for gig tickets. If you know you can get 200 to come along to a gig and you book a venue that only holds 150, you're probably going to get people waiting outside to try and get in. This all helps create a feeling of being in-demand. It's all a perception thing because if you put those same 150 people in a 1,000 person venue, the perception would be that you'd not done very well. Deliberately limiting creates exclusivity. When you say there's only 5 of something left, everybody wants one. Being sold out also gives you a great marketing story. I've run ads many times saying that an event's sold out. People think I'm mad but I'm marketing the brand for the *next* event, building the perception that it's not to be missed. And the next event will be even busier because everyone will get in faster. If someone tells you that you can't have something it makes you want it even more. It's basic psychology. And this creates the drip-drip effect of always being sold out. I can't think of anything this principle wouldn't work with, even teaching.

When I used to give guitar lessons I'd ask people to tell me the time that worked for them for a lesson, then I'd tell them that they were lucky because it was the only slot I'd got left. If people think you're in high demand they'll move heaven and earth to make it on time. If they think you're always available they might not take you so seriously. Whenever someone rang up to enquire about The Indie Killers, the sales agent's first reaction would be, 'you'll be lucky'. Then, when she found a slot, she'd say, 'oh that's weird, they're actually free on X date.' We'd get booked instantly because she'd created the perception that we were never free and they'd be lucky to get us. This all taps into the "I was there" moment. People want to be part of the exclusive club who heard about the next big thing first. Nobody wants to settle for second best.

Social media

My first book, *The Rule Breaker's Guide to Social Media*, is all about how you can use social media to build your audience and take control of your career as a musician. With the music industry changing on a regular basis, musicians need to build and monetise their brand. Anyone who knows me or follows my channels will have heard me talk a lot about this. In today's climate, the musician or band who builds an engaged fan-base holds the power, and social media is still the Holy Grail when it comes to building and looking after your audience.

But social media is an ever-changing thing. It's been less than a year since my first book came out but there have been several evolutions within the social platforms since. The noticeable difference is that the constant algorithm changes mean musicians need to put out more content at a higher level to cut through the noise AND find the budget to distribute that content regularly. It's no longer a debate about whether to spend money on distributing content, it's now a necessity. The glory days when it was all free are over, sadly. In spite of this, social media still offers the whole package in marketing terms as far as I'm concerned. You can show yourself off, talk to your audience, find out more about your audience, advertise and rally the troops in order to make money or get people to a gig.

> *One thing I would say is that the pillar system is more important than ever before.*

The pillar system involves creating a piece of content which can be broken down into smaller and smaller pieces. For example, once a week I film the #AskDamo Show as a way of bringing value to musicians. I pick four questions from my audience and answer them in a 30 minute video hosted on YouTube. That show can then be broken down into four smaller videos – one per question – to put on Facebook and YouTube. These will be broken down further into one minute videos for my Insta feed. While the show's being recorded we have a live feeds going out on Facebook and Instagram. Then I'll give the show to a writer to transcribe into four blogs – one per question. I'll also strip the audio, which can go out on SoundCloud and Spotify. One of my staff will listen to the show to pick out twenty key phrases, which could be put into tweets and possibly Instagram Stories. Then finally, I'll re-purpose one or two of the blogs and a video for LinkedIn. In a nutshell, from one piece of 30 minute content created on a Wednesday, I can get enough content for the whole week.

Here's an example of how you could make the pillar system work for you, using a gig as the pillar. You could make a vlog-style video of the whole day. You could film a backstage warm-up song. You could have a live Q&A from backstage and potentially a couple of mini backstage photo shoots. You could get someone to film part of the gig. Once you've got all of your content from the day you can break it down into potentially 20 or 30 pieces of content to put out across all of your platforms. It's not just about the content you make but how you break it down and re-purpose it that counts. There are so many different ways to share content, and you need to be putting out a lot of content to try and get around the pesky algorithm.

Social media is so big and daunting people often don't know where to start... so they don't. If you feel a bit overwhelmed by it all, start by creating a couple of weekly pillars to help keep you on track. My weekly pillars are the #AskDamo Show and my weekly challenge. Knowing I've got these two pillars in place helps me feel on top of my social media and, if I don't have the time to create any extra content, it doesn't matter because I know I'll have enough for the week. Social media can be a bit like song-writing – if you leave it to inspiration it often doesn't come. You need to force yourself to create regularly regardless. Having this kind of structure and routine is important for your followers too, it helps them feel connected to you.

Show off every aspect of what you do

The great thing is, a lot of your content doesn't need to be overly thought out or created from scratch because you can simply document what you're doing. Musicians tend to forget that they're already doing lots of things that could be marketed. Every rehearsal, gig and band meeting, every new riff, every studio day, every build up to a tour. There are stories to be told in all of these things – all you need to do is recognise the opportunity. I always ask bands to take a picture with their audience at every gig they do because it tells the story of the night. If you've had a great gig and get everyone involved in the picture it can go right across your social media. The same thing applies at rehearsals. You could take a picture of the band and record the final ten minutes of rehearsal in order to have some footage for your socials. If you're having a band meeting, come up with a creative way of documenting the story of that meeting. If you've written a new song, show a clip from it to get people invested in it right from the start. If the first your audience hear of a new song is when you're launching it, you're beginning with the end of the story.

A band I follow once made a post about one of their members leaving, explaining that there were no hard feeling and he was leaving due to artistic differences. I was so interested in this story and I really wanted to know what was going to happen next. Most bands wouldn't do this, they'd only tell their audience what had happened when their new member was in place. If you document your band life regularly you get people involved from the beginning of each separate story and you take them with you on the journey. As you can probably see, all of this revolves around how good you are at telling stories – not just the story of the day but how it fits in with the bigger story of you as a band or musician. YouTubers are great at this, so try watching successful vloggers for tips on how to tell a story.

Imagine if there was footage of Freddie Mercury sitting down with the rest of Queen, saying, 'I've got a new idea for a song' and then he started playing them *Bohemian Rhapsody*. Imagine if we could see the look on their faces. Imagine seeing footage of Nirvana jamming ideas for *Teen Spirit*. We can now do that for our audience but we choose not to. The main reason for this is because we're fearful that what we're working on won't be any good. But what if it is? Or what if, after hours of struggling, you get that eureka moment and what started off sounding dodgy ends up sounding amazing. How great would it be for your audience to share in that journey?

Once again, it all comes down to the amount of content you make and capture and the more you take people with you and allow them in. Trust me, people really want to see the real-life goings on behind the scenes. Why do you think shows like *Big Brother* are so popular? We're all really nosey!

Part Eight: Money

This is probably going to be the most controversial part of this book and cause more than a few people to get on their high horse. It's a hot topic because whenever money's involved, the value of you and your work is in question. This part of the book is about cutting through the bullshit and getting you to the point where you're a tradeable commodity in the eyes of the people who count in this business, rather than friends and family, who will always tell you you're worth something. At the end of the day, it's all about supply and demand, and increasing the demand for what you do because that gives you leverage. In this section we're going to look at removing the *woulda coulda shoulda* and focus instead on increasing your leverage and standing out from the competition.

You wouldn't expect a plumber...

'You wouldn't expect a plumber to do a job for exposure,' is a line a lot of musicians use. I have a bit of an issue with this. Firstly, why is it always a plumber? It's the worst example going. Your job is to stand on stage and have people adore you. A plumber's job is to stick their hand down a toilet full of shit. Of course you wouldn't expect them to do that for free or next to no money. The trouble with a lot of musicians is that they get to a certain level and their ego kicks in. We're back to the old chestnut of not appreciating what a privilege it is to be a professional musician. It's interesting that so many feel they'd be lowering themselves to play for free. That said, when you deserve to get paid for your skill because you are in demand it's a completely different issue.

> *I'm not saying art should be free, as it absolutely shouldn't; the key is in recognising when free works to your advantage and when your leverage makes you worth being paid.*

I understand that musicians need to earn a living like anyone else but I'd also say that if you're not getting paid, there's a reason for that and your job is to discover that reason and change or improve it. I don't have any trouble getting paid to play now because I have a lot of experience. If I'm asked to do something for free I can afford to decide whether or not I want to. However, if at any point my phone stops ringing and I stop getting offers, I'll know I need to figure out what has changed and what I can do to fix things, and the best way I can do that is to get out there and play for free and network and improve.

People make the mistake of believing that you should only do free gigs at the beginning of your career but the harsh reality is you might have to do it again later down the line because the industry changes so fast. A great example of this happened in 2008 when the recession hit and people could no longer afford to splash out on ten-piece disco and funk bands for their parties. I was 30 at the time; a slightly uncool chubby bass player who could play funk. If I wanted to survive in the business I realised I had to rethink my strategy, potentially retrain and learn how to sing, lower my prices and create a whole new kind of band. And that's exactly what I did, starting my three-piece rock band, The Indie Killers. I wasn't too proud to start all over again from scratch and because of that we went on to build a really profitable career.

Too many musicians reach a certain age and think it's their divine right to carry on at the level they've reached forever. If a young musician comes along and undercuts or out-markets them they see it as being hugely unfair, complaining that they're dragging the price down to the bottom. This is crap because you can always charge more for experience and a proven track record. I'm not worried about some kid coming along and charging half the price I do. If they try and charge the same as me it's even more laughable. The fact is, at some point in the future someone will come along who's better looking, a better player and prepared to do twice as much work for half the price you do. The question is, what are you going to do about it?

Musicians might be quick to dismiss playing for exposure but there's no denying that it's a tradeable commodity and it's all relative. It's up to you to decide if the value of the exposure matches up to the value of the work. Something might not pay off immediately but it will ultimately. Every gig is an asset for your CV. Your job is to build up the assets until you don't need any more.

The power of free

'The power of free' is something I say a lot and musicians don't like it, but it's about knowing your worth and being realistic. It's about supply and demand and most importantly leverage. The first thing to realise is that there are a lot of musicians desperate for a shot at the title. And because there is so much supply and a much, much smaller amount of demand, it means the strongest will survive. You're owed nothing at the start of your career. So, in order to build your leverage, you need to be good and in order to get good you need to put in the hours. In his book *Outliers: The Story of Success*, author Malcolm Gladwell claims that it takes 10,000 hours of doing something to become an expert at it. This very well may be true, but you need to pay attention to the specifics. If you spend 10,000 hours in your bedroom practising, you'll become an expert at practising. If you spend that time on stage, you'll become an expert at performing. Musicians tend to confuse the two, but they're very different things. The same applies for recording in the studio and teaching and songwriting – all of those things are their own specialist area. The power of doing things for free in your early career is that it helps you build your experience and therefore your value in that area. As I've said before, with over 2,000 gigs under my belt, I'm now an expert as a gigging musician. But having only been in the studio 50-60 times, I'm capable but nowhere near an expert in that environment. Therefore pricing my worth as the same for both would be silly.

> *Use the power of free to help you increase your worth as a musician.*

See it as a long-term investment and don't be too proud or egotistical to realise how it can benefit you.

After posting a video on this subject on my YouTube channel, I was left this comment from a guy called Mikael: *'Your advice is typically good, but in this case you're only painting half the picture and your examples are absurd. I can't think of any situation in which one would be asked to open for the Foo Fighters or play on a professionally produced album without getting paid to do so. Yes, exposure is good in some situations. If I was asked to perform for free in front of a room full of music supervisors or event planners (people who could actually further my career) of course I would do it. But usually you're being asked to play for "exposure" in situations where that exposure would never help you to further your career'.*

This was my reply: *'Hi Mikael, out of all my videos I think this is one I stand by more than almost any of them and I can give many examples. The biggest gig I performed at was Hyde Park in front of 150,000 people. I spent the week performing with Alanis, Clapton, I even played with Taylor Hawkins. Guess how much I got paid... Yep zero. Last year I performed at 18 stadium gigs as a contract for Sky Sports – Newcastle, Swansea, Bolton, Leeds etc. I was offered petrol money only and I took it because as I expected, it led to probably another 50 gigs off the back of it. It's all about leverage and if it's not worth it we can always say no. But the reason why I have always had 3 times too many paid gigs than I needed was because I built up leverage and then traded it in other areas. Sky Sports didn't need me, but once I had played 18 stadiums in 12 months, more people wanted me and I cashed it in. Like you say, many times musicians get asked to play for exposure and the leverage isn't worth it and we can decline those offers, however many musicians lose out because they have too much ego to play for free and some of those decisions could have built them a bigger career should they have grasped onto the opportunity. ☺ There is nothing wrong with plumbers, I just think musicians give them a bad rap lol. Damo.'*

Knowing your worth

If you want to have a career as a musician and you're not performing regularly on a Saturday night (the easiest night of the week to get gigs) you have no right to complain about not getting paid for gigs. Over the course of my last five years as a gigging musician I missed about seven Saturday gigs, and those would have been during the most off-peak season or down to a cancellation. From a supply and demand point of view, once you're in this much demand you're able to charge. But if you only gig periodically, you're not in as much demand as you need to be to charge fully. Consistently making a living as a musician over a period of years is hard.

> *In order to do so you need to make yourself in demand and the best way to do that is to gig for free until you don't have to.*

In doing free gigs you're building your experience, not just as a live performer but in setting up, admin and what to say, wear and do. You're also building a network of contacts and people are slowly figuring out that you're worth getting on their gigs. You're building your stock and net worth as a musician. So, when people phone you up to ask you to play for them, you can charge. If they're not doing that, look around for opportunities to gig simply to get your name out there and build your experience.

When it comes to your worth and how much you can charge there's usually a steady trajectory. At some point you'll find that you'll be able to charge during the busy seasons like summer but you'll still find it hard to get paid gigs off-peak, when there are less gigs available. My advice would be to take on free gigs during those times. Fill your diary with anything you can get – open mic nights, local pub gigs – right up until the point where the paid gigs are coming in so frequently you don't have to do any more for free.

As I said before, the more gigs you do, the more you'll be building your worth as a musician. You want to get so good that people will see you as the safest pair of hands and best option out there. This is a principle I apply to everything I do work-wise. When I started keynote speaking I paid for myself to turn up and do talks for free. I recognised that I needed the experience, I needed people to see me speaking and I needed the social proofing for my online platforms. Keynote speaking was an area I wanted to get into so badly I was prepared to do it for free and pay all of my travel expenses – even when one of the talks I did was in Boston! I did a bunch of talks like this, then I started getting offered travel expenses. Then I started getting paid small amounts like £200 to speak. But I know that if I keep building my worth as a speaker, within a couple of years I'll be paid between £5,000 and £10,000 per talk. But there's no way I'll get to that point without the foundation of the power of free. So often, musicians talk about working for free like it's this disgusting thing, which I find really weird. You're not only building your experience and worth but you're getting to do something you love. When I go on speaking gigs I view them as adventures. Do the same with your gigs. Love it and enjoy it. It's all building value and leading to money. Focus on the positives.

So, how do you know when to charge? Well, just because we're recognising the power of free in order to learn and gain experience, there's no harm in asking for money. Do your research and figure out what other prices are being charged in your market and then be realistic. People will expect to pay more for the experience of Ash Soan on drums, as he performed on Adele's albums and is the house drummer for *The Voice UK*, just as they will expect to pay less for a recent music college graduate who is keen but inexperienced.

If you are regularly getting rejected when you are bringing up money, you're probably charging more than you're worth at the moment but if you can't remember the last time you were offered a gig, let alone asked how much, do the math! The Musicians Union will tell you the industry standard, but take that with a pinch of salt, because that figure is an average of everything that's being charged right across the board. Say the Musician's Union rate for a guitar teacher is £33 per hour – that fails to take other key factors such as location into consideration. You can't charge the same price in Stoke that you do in Kensington. Similarly, if you're an experienced musician with a number one album to your name, you can charge more as a teacher than a student fresh out of college with a BTEC. Age, experience, location, competition in the area, all go into determining your worth.

Investing in yourself

There's a common misconception that investing in yourself will cost money but there are so many ways you can invest in yourself without spending a penny. Investing in your knowledge and education can be totally free, especially nowadays with the amount of YouTube tutorials and educational blog-posts available. Investing in yourself is all about asking, *how can I make myself more employable today than I was yesterday?* It's about seeing yourself as an asset, an asset that keeps growing. For example, improving your playing.

Image is something that often goes under the radar from an investment point of view. I hear so many musicians say things like, 'take me as I am, image doesn't matter, Ed Sheeran's ginger and he still got to number one' (don't worry, some of my best friends are ginger). But, as I said in the section on gigging, image is definitely an area of self improvement and it's an area I struggled with. Bruce always used to say to me, 'You could do yourself a huge favour by sorting out an image rather than just wearing clothes.'

> *Creating a strong image or look is a great investment because it will make you memorable and take you further.*

As I said before, and I'm sure I'll say it again, music is a fashion-based industry.

Another key way to invest in yourself is to pay close attention to changes in the industry and consumption. You need to respect that traditions are not rules and they will change. By paying attention and remaining flexible you're investing in one of your biggest assets – your brain. Nurture it and fill it with knowledge.

There are so many ways you can invest in yourself. Invest in your mental health with a meditation routine. Invest in your physical health by exercising regularly. Have some business coaching. Allocating specific time in your diary to learning and bettering yourself is a sure-fire way of increasing your chances of success. Create your own tailor-made curriculum, allocating two or three hours of uninterrupted time to the area you want to study. It could be online advertising. It could be learning how to edit videos so you can be more productive with your content. It could be music production so you can produce your own demos. By allocating a set number of hours per week to your study think how good you'd get in a year. You'd be an expert.

Ed Sheeran is a great example of someone who really invested in his music career. You can track his progression online from clips of his first demos. He didn't just pop up perfectly formed, he put the time and effort in, to such an extent that he spent almost two years sleeping on friends' sofas in order to pursue his dream. Any money he got went into his career and art. He did open mic nights and collabs at every opportunity, in order to play and learn and get known. At the time of writing this book his net worth is somewhere around $100 million. I'm not advocating jacking everything in and making the ultimate gamble. But Sheeran's the perfect example of someone who took his outgoings right down to the bare minimum in order to invest in his music. And regardless of what you might think of his music, there's no doubt that his dedication to his craft is an inspiration.

How many gigs should you be doing a year?

Carrying on from the power of free, if you make your goal the number of gigs you play rather than the amount of money earned you'll be more successful. Having a target of 120 gigs a year is definitely doable. I know because I've done it year on year. Supposing you do 50% of them for free in the first year. By the third or fourth year you should be being paid for all of them because of the momentum you'll have gained. However, if you're holding out for a certain amount of money you'll probably only do about 30 gigs a year. Yes, they'll all be paid but the growth will be slower. Whilst everyone is different I think a full time musician should be gigging twice a week. And frankly, if you don't want to gig 100 times a year you're in the wrong industry. Why would you not want the buzz and enjoyment of playing 100 times?

It's important to note here that it really is OK if you don't want to do it. I can vividly remember the moment I fell out of love with gigging. I was standing on stage and the drummer kicked into the song *Walking on Sunshine*. I'd spent years with a bass in my hand working on my chops, trying to sweet pick Yngwie Malmsteen solos, only to be standing on stage playing three notes. I love bass playing but this was not what I'd dreamed of doing, and I thought to myself, *that's it, I'm done, I don't want to do this anymore*. After that gig I didn't pick up the bass for two years.

See your day job as an investor in your dream

On the #AskDamoShow the questions are different every week, but there's a certain theme running though most of them, and that is: *how do you... sell records/promote your band/get gigs... when you don't have any money?* There's a good reason musicians are thought of as always being skint, it's a tough industry. The flip side of having more control than ever over your career is that it comes at a price. Literally. To take full control of your career you need your own transport, the right gear, a portable studio and the ability to promote yourself online, which is now costing more.

Acknowledging the expense involved is the first step, the second is finding the money to finance your dream. If you don't have the Bank of Mum and Dad to rely on you'll need a steady source of income to support your addiction to creation. It's up to you whether you get this source of income from a completely separate job, or from something within the music industry, like teaching or working in a covers band. After my first band failed I got a job in a shampoo factory. It lasted for four hours – the time it took me to realise that I had to earn my living from music in some way. Because of that I was quite happy to go into the world of covers bands, being paid to play for whoever, whatever, whenever. A musical gun for hire, if you like. If someone offered me a gig back then I'd be there like shot, in order to get out and play, get better at my playing and get money. I'm not saying I made a fortune; when I was 19 we played a residency every Thursday for £90 for the three of us, working out at a grant total of £30 each. And I'm not so ancient that £30 was loads of money back then, you couldn't exactly buy a house with it. But it was money and more importantly, a way of building more money from doing what I loved.

> *If you're serious about your musical ambitions you need to be regularly putting money aside to fund your dream and you need to treat this as seriously as you do your taxes.*

Imagine if you automatically 'taxed' yourself 10% of everything you earn, which went straight into a pot to fund your music career. Imagine if, just like income tax, it was illegal not to pay into this fund. If you had to find it you would. You could set up a separate account into which you pay a monthly direct debit. If you can't currently afford to put aside 10% of your income for your music, how about getting a second, part-time job, like working in a bar or cafe three hours a week, so that you can put every penny of that income into your musical progression?

If, after reading all of this, you're still saying, 'I don't have the money to put into my music career,' you have two choices – rein in your expectations or just do it for fun.

Sacrifice for the long-term

We've never lived in a time where so many things have been available on demand, at just the click of a button. We're now used to getting things as soon as we want them and this attitude can spill into our career aspirations too. But what you have to understand is that success in the music industry doesn't come instantly and without sacrifice.

> *The reality is, success takes time and costs energy and it's all about the focus.*

If you genuinely want success as badly as you say you do then you need to become tunnel vision focused, with your eyes firmly on the prize. You will need to sacrifice certain things from your life in order to save money, time and energy.

The list of things you might have to sacrifice for success in your music career is endless. Everything from downsizing your property so you pay less in rent, to selling instruments you don't need, and even how much time you spend on Tinder. And I'm being deadly serious about this last one – the amount of energy people put into getting laid these days is astonishing. How can you focus on anything else if your phone is pinging away all the time? Getting laid takes up valuable time, energy and money!

Try doing a tally of how much time you typically spend on Netflix, social media and apps like Tinder. There's nothing wrong with doing these things but if you're not prepared to sacrifice the amount of time, money and energy spent, be prepared to lower your career expectations. Imagine if you turned your phone off from for a few hours every day, to allow you to focus on your music. You'd get loads done. I know it seems hard to believe but it wasn't all that long ago that no-one had mobile phones and we all survived. I regularly turn the notifications off on my phone so that I can focus on my work and it makes a huge difference.

Teaching vs covers as supplementary income

People tend to look at covers work and teaching as an either or thing but I think they complement each other really well as an income source. As I said earlier in this section, when I walked out of my job at the shampoo factory in Swansea I knew I had to make a living from music and a friend of mine introduced me to covers bands. But the problem with covers work is that it's very seasonal. The peak seasons are the summer, when people want bands for parties, company award ceremonies and weddings, and at Christmas, when there are loads of corporate gigs, parties and a fair few weddings too. Unfortunately, when January, February and March come around, nobody wants to party. Similarly, at the end of summer everything dies off a bit.

For this reason I think it can be really helpful to see teaching as something that can supplement your work in the covers world, or vice versa. The great thing about music teaching is that it's seasonal too, but the peak seasons in teaching conveniently fall during the quietest times for the covers industry. As soon as school starts back in September people want lessons again. It's the same in the winter. Loads of people get a new instrument for Christmas and want to start lessons in the new year.

Teaching and covers bands work hand in hand. Whilst it might not earn you enough to buy you a Ferrari, if you're gigging seventy times a year in a covers band and teaching fifteen hours a week, you'll probably make about £25 – 30k per year. Enough to pay the bills and have some money left over to build your main focus career. It will also really help to improve your playing because you'll have your instrument in your hand pretty much every day. And another bonus of this kind of work is that it buys you time because gigs tend to be at the weekend and lessons in the evenings, giving you the day time during the week to work on you the artist, band and musician.

> *As far as I'm concerned, teaching and covers don't just provide you with a bread and butter income, they provide you with the perfect opportunity to improve, fund yourself and give you the time needed to work on your main hustle.*

Learning how to set up and market a covers band when I was 19 was hugely instrumental in me being able to set up BIMM. One made £10,000 per year while the other is worth £60 million, but the fundamentals are the same. You're learning basic business skills at the same time as improving your music, and you're still working in the area you love. It surprises me when I hear musicians say they'd never work in a covers band but they'd happily work in a bank or McDonalds. I don't get how this is the better option, when it offers you so much less in terms of invaluable experience. People have this misguided idea that playing in a covers band is cheesy and soul destroying. But as I said earlier in this book, my last covers band played at 18 stadiums in a 12 month period, as part of a contract with Sky TV. I also know a guitar teacher who's built an online following on YouTube and gets paid £5,000 per video on monthly retainers. I know another guitar teacher who turns over well over a million per year because he's advanced from one-to-one to online teaching. It all started with teaching kids in his spare room.

Stop selling music

As I explained in detail in the Introduction to this book, back in the day, if you wanted to buy a piece of music you would have to physically get up and go out and buy an actual product, such as a record or a cassette tape or a CD. But things have changed, and they've changed dramatically. Music no longer needs to be attached to a physical product. Now we can download or stream any track or album we want on our phone. The horse has bolted and we need to stop trying to close the stable door. The harsh reality is, we are living in a time when music is priceless but worthless. What do I mean by that? Certain tracks will always be priceless in terms of how much they mean to you. When I heard *Enter Sandman* by Metallica for the first time as a kid, it changed everything for me. As I stood there watching the video on MTV, I knew there and then that I wanted to be a musician. That track changed my life, so it will always be priceless to me, but how much would I pay for it today? Nothing. I have a Spotify subscription which allows me to play anything.

> *The fact is, the negatives of trying to sell music by far outweigh the positives.*

To recap, here's why I think we should stop selling music...

1. If you're telling your audience to buy your tracks on iTunes and stream for free, you're going to confuse them. You need one clear message – tell them where to stream it. Simple.
2. You're confusing your targets. Instead of trying to achieve goals in four different areas and spreading yourself too thinly, focus on doing one thing incredibly well.
3. In trying to sell music, you are defying consumption – the numbers don't lie. People are not buying music, so don't force it down their throats.

I'm not saying you shouldn't sell CDs or vinyl at your shows, but I would class this as selling merch rather than music and it's never going to be a huge revenue stream. Ultimately, I think you'd be far better off getting your music out there and building your audience via streaming and focusing on monetising your brand through deals and collabs.

Part Nine: Life Lessons

This chapter contains all the things I wish people had told me when I was starting out – the things that that have made the biggest positive difference to my music career. The fact is, there's so much work out there for musicians but they just don't realise it. This chapter isn't so much about how to get work, it's more about what's stopping you from getting it. And a major factor in this is realising how little competition there actually is out there, if you take your career seriously. Basically, if you change your mindset it's like turning on a tap and the work will come flooding in. Think of this chapter as turning on that tap.

The importance of driving

I get into a lot of trouble for telling musicians they should drive but to me, driving is the cornerstone of your early musical career, a crucial factor in your ability to get work. As a musician you spend large chunks of your life travelling, in either trains, planes, cars or buses, to as many as 200 different places a year. When you're starting out and before you hit the big time you have to organise that travel yourself. There's only so many times you can call on favours from friends, family and partners to take you to a gig. If I wasn't able to drive I wouldn't have been able to have a career in a music and the same is true for you, especially if you don't live in a major city.

People get really stubborn when they don't drive and they make excuses. But learning to drive and buying a car really isn't that big a deal. I understand that there are some exceptions to this rule; if you can't drive due to a disability, for example. But this book is all about being brutally honest and the truth is, not having your own transport will hamper your career and slow you down. For most people this is an easy fix and a quick win. Sometimes musicians will tell me that they'll get a car once they're doing enough gigs. But I think it should be the other way round. If you get the car you'll get more gigs.

Anytime someone is looking for a dep (a last minute replacement for a musician who's sick) they'll need someone who can get themselves to a gig. Every dep you do is an opportunity to get more work. Therefore, if you don't have a car you won't be able to get to the gigs and you won't get more work. But if you build a reputation as someone who is self sufficient you'll get the work.

About two years ago I got a message on social media from a girl who was a guitarist. She looked amazing, with bright red hair the colour of a fire engine, and she was such a great player. In short, she was extremely marketable. I was really surprised when she told me she couldn't find work, then I found out that she couldn't drive. When I told her that she needed to learn to drive in order to get gigs she was hesitant. A few days later I got a call from a friend who's a fixer for a bunch of TV shows including *The X Factor*, looking for a female guitarist. I phoned the girl and explained what an amazing opportunity this would be, playing with big names on TV on a regular basis. However, one of the stipulations of the job was that she had to be able to drive to the gigs. She made a massive fuss about this and didn't get the job, which was a shame because it was hers for the taking.

About two months later she came back to me asking if I could put her forward for more work. She still couldn't drive and told me that she didn't have the time or money to learn, so I said I wouldn't be able to find her any work, to which she replied, 'I guess I could get my mum to teach me. She's a driving instructor.' My response to this was something along the lines of, 'Are you fucking kidding me?!' I couldn't believe it. She had the option of free lessons all along but didn't bother taking them and lost a major, career-making gig. Within six months her CV would have been amazing, but she threw it away purely because of her stubbornness. I understand that some people might have a genuine fear of driving, but if you want to succeed you need to try and overcome that fear. It really could be a game-changer.

Taking the rough with the smooth

Life as a musician is probably more inconsistent than any other industry I can think of. In professional sport you are what you are – if you're the best you're the best. But with music you can have amazing CV-changing moments and then the next day it all goes back to normal. Being a musician is always a case of asking *what next?* You have to be able to take the rough with the smooth. If you want a career (and I'm not talking about getting work here, I'm talking about building a 40 or 50 year career) you'd better believe that the highs will be high and the lows will be low – and they might even happen within a week of each other!

Here's an example of how I've had to take the rough with the smooth in my own life as a musician. When I was 19 I was asked to perform at the Monsters of Rock concert at Hyde Park, which at the time was the largest concert that had ever been put on in the UK. The concept of the gig was tomorrow's stars playing alongside today's monsters of rock, in front of 150,000 people. I was one of the lucky musicians considered one of the stars of tomorrow, which meant I was playing alongside the likes of Eric Clapton, Bob Dylan, Alanis Morissette, Jools Holland and The Who. In the lead-up to the gig there was a national press tour for a week, which entailed hanging out and playing with these superstars in some form or another in hotels and studios. You'd walk into a room have a jam with Alanis Morissette and Roger Daltrey then have an interview with them. For an entire week we were driven around in armoured cars with security and all of these famous people. A pinnacle moment for me was where we had to sound check on stage. Eric Clapton was a couple of feet to one side of me and Pete Townsend was a couple of feet the other way, and next to him was Dave Gilmour and over in the corner was Gary Glitter... But it's probably best not to mention him. At one point I turned round and behind me Taylor Hawkins – the second best drummer in the Foo Fighters – was fiddling with his drums. The next day we played together in front of 150,000 people. The standout moment was playing *Pinball Wizard*. I was 19 years old and Pete Townsend was ten feet away from me. I remember thinking, *can my life get any better*, as I looked out at 150,000 people going crazy.

Fast forward three days and I was standing on stage at a gig in a social club – the Lightwater CIU just outside of Guildford to be specific. I was playing with midi-file backing tracks to an audience of about five people, three of whom were working behind the bar. As the keyboard intro to *Pinball Wizard* started I remember thinking, *can my life get any worse*? At exactly that moment a little old lady walked over to the stage and leant forward to say something. I thought it was going to be a request for a song but she asked if we could turn it down as they were about to start playing bingo. I instantly thought to myself, *yes it can and has got worse*. The irony is, I got paid more for the social club gig than I did for Hyde Park but that's the way it goes. The golden nugget of wisdom here is that I got asked to play the Hyde Park gig because I'd played hundreds of horrific social club gigs by then. I was the safest pair of hands at that age for the gig.

Moral of the story: you don't get the smooth without a lot of the rough.

Becoming unstoppable or irreplaceable

There are so many ways you can make yourself hireable as a musician – and a big part of that is acknowledging that there's a lot less money in the music industry than there once was. Because so much music is available for free on the likes of YouTube and SoundCloud, we've seen labels and their budgets shrink rapidly. And budgets have *really* shrunk at the lower end of the music industry. There's less money for musicians and songwriters than there ever used to be. Twenty years ago, making an album in the studio would have required four to six weeks recording time at a very expensive studio rate. The same was true with touring; there were lavish budgets because the tours wouldn't just sell tickets, they'd sell albums. Effectively they'd promote each other. But this is no longer the case. Because of this, your job is to make yourself more hireable than the next musician. For example, a lot of bands can no longer afford to take backing vocalists on tour, so they'll look for a guitarist or bass player who can sing. Here are some simple steps you can take to instantly make yourself more hireable...

- Learn to sing
- Learn a second instrument. If you're a guitarist learn the bass as well as some keyboard, so you can pad out the sound live if needed
- Bass players should add some synth to their game because that's where the market is
- If you're a drummer, learn to do backing vocals – a drummer who can sing will definitely find work.

Depping is a big problem. Too many musicians want the free and easy, lack of commitment life and jump out of a gig so they can take a better offer. They want a non-committal set-up but imagine if it was a relationship. Imagine if your partner said to you, 'We're kind of together but if someone hotter comes along I'll go off with him tonight and see you tomorrow.' Why would someone be committed to you if you're not committed to them?

Another way you can make yourself irreplaceable is to understand sound. Too many young musicians of today don't understand sound the way musicians of old did, and by that I mean people before my time. Understanding how to set up a PA, how to get a good sound for the band and even owning a PA all make you more irreplaceable. If you're standing in a venue made of stone and glass and you're able to tell the rest of the band, 'I know how to get the best sound out of this venue,' they'll feel like they're in safe hands and they won't want to lose that. They won't want to lose you.

> *The moral of this section is that, while it's fantastic that you're a specialist in your field as a musician, in the current climate with others clambering for gigs I would ask, what else do you bring to the party?*

A recession might be around the corner, or a drop in album or ticket sales. You don't want to be the first one to be replaced. Think in terms of football teams and their irreplaceable players – the ones the manager would never willingly put up for transfer. That's who you want to be, through your playing, additional skills and positive attitude. It all goes into making you that bit more irreplaceable.

Finding the positives

Every gig I've done, no matter how badly it's gone or how much hard work it's been, I've always been massively appreciative of the big picture, which is that I get to perform as a musician. I wish I could get more musicians to realise what a privilege it is to do that for a living, especially if you compare it to other jobs, like being a bin man or digging up roads. I'm not saying that it's not hard work being a musician, but you have to appreciate that so many people work really hard at things they hate. Working hard at something you love is a privilege. I'm convinced that's one of the main reasons I've had so many gigs – because I keep a really positive attitude about it.

We used to have a drummer who made it very clear that he was only there for the money. He didn't really want to do it and so he started having quite a negative impact on the rest of the band. As I've already covered in this book, life on the road can be a very tough thing. You need people around you who will make it fun to compensate for the pressures. If you're not in it for the right reasons, if you don't appreciate the privilege, it will rub off on everyone else and they won't want to be around you. A negative or money-grabbing attitude will definitely affect your ability to get work, so learn to take the rough with the smooth and keep a positive attitude.

Take a few seconds now and seriously think about it. Do you truly appreciate what a privilege it is to be a musician? It's easy to be blasé about it. But if you were born into a life of famine and poverty you'd have a very different attitude. Think of all the war-torn parts of the world you could have been born into and the opportunities you might have been denied, in spite of your talents. Looking at it this way can help give you a fresh and more positive perspective.

Another thing that can help to maintain a positive attitude is to keep coming back to why you're doing this in the first place – your love of music. Having a regular creative outlet helps to keep it fun and will see you through the harder aspects. So many musicians self-destruct because they lose their love for music. It's so important to find ways to keep that love alive.

Continual learning helps too. Most musicians are at their happiest when they're developing and growing. A common mistake is to reach a certain level and stop trying. But then it gets boring. Lady Gaga is a great example of an artist who's always trying to extend herself and be the best she can be, by evolving, experimenting and learning.

When I was working at BIMM, I lost my love for playing. I'd always vowed that if I fell out of love with playing I'd stop immediately, so that's what I did. I pulled out of the bands I was in and stopped gigging for three years. I was lucky that I was able to do this financially because I was building BIMM. But BIMM was also part of the reason I lost the passion, because I wasn't putting any creativity and learning into my playing. When you stop learning and growing as a musician it's like playing the same level of a video game again and again and again.

> *A simple exercise you can do right now to help you find the positives in your own musical career is to write a list of ten things you love about being a musician.*

It's a great way of reminding yourself why you got into the game in the first place.

The art of control

When I look back on my life as a musician I can see that the number one reason for me having a successful career, with non-stop gigs, is that I've taken full control of my career. Whether it's been through learning to drive so I can get myself to gigs or making myself irreplaceable in other ways, I've made it my mission to proactively build my career rather than bump along hoping for the best. The sooner a musician realises that their career is solely down to them and the decisions they make, the sooner they'll succeed.

A lot of musicians want to jump into a winning band without really having to work for it. But if you're just turning up and getting paid to play, you're always at risk of being replaced. And if you're in a band and you can see reasons why something isn't going to be successful, including other members of the band, and you don't do anything about it, you'll probably fail.

The art of taking control of your musical career is a bit like tick boxes. Ask yourself, *what are the things that can stop me having a career and what can I do to solve those problems?* Supposing one of those issues is finding the money to fund your band. Taking control would be putting a covers band together or starting a teaching practise to raise some money.

Whether you like it or not, musicians have to be slightly entrepreneurial nowadays. You have to find ways to create and build something and market it to get results. Whether it's an album, a covers band or a teaching business, they all rely on entrepreneurial spirit and your career will live or die by the decisions you make. Musicians need to realise that if something doesn't work, it's on them to find the solutions.

One of the biggest issues you can face is when one or more of your bandmates aren't pulling their weight. I understand that you want to be loyal to them but ask yourself if they're really being loyal to you. It has to work both ways. Imagine if, a couple of years down the line, their lack of commitment causes the band to break up. It would be all too easy to blame them but if you knew they were slacking and did nothing about it, the responsibility lies with you too. Obviously try and help them if there's a genuine issue but if they still won't pull their weight you need to sack them or leave. It's similar to being the boss of a company. If someone in my company makes a mistake it's ultimately my responsibility because I hired and trained them and gave them the autonomy to make decisions. The buck always tops with me because I have to take responsibility for my actions.

Maybe this section has made you think of something that's been niggling at you that isn't quite right – a band member, or your time management, or a relationship that's stopping you from getting to where you want to go. The art of control is all about identifying the problem and coming up with the solution. If you don't and it all goes wrong you only have yourself to blame.

> *Write a list of all the issues you face right now as a musician. Then write another list of the steps you could take to address and overcome them.*

Doing this exercise will immediately help you to feel more in control.

Don't be a dick

Due to the internet and modern technology, the world is more transparent than it's ever been. Social media in particular has made everything so visible. Therefore, if you act like a dick, you're way more likely to be found out and your career is way more likely to suffer as a consequence. One thing that no-one tells you at music college is that you never know where the people you meet on your musical journey might end up. You might be in college or playing in a local community band with the next Ed Sheeran. People have long memories, especially if you act like a dick. As the old saying goes, 'be nice to the people on your way up; you'll meet the same people on the way down.'

There are multiple ways to be a dick in the music world. It's not just other musicians you should treat with respect. So many musicians fail to treat the sound guys with the respect they deserve because they're too caught up in their own egos. At the end of the day, the sound crew are there to make you sound good. If you ignore them or are rude to them you're effectively shutting down opportunities to put on a better performance, as well as being a dick. A simple 'please' and 'thank you' goes a long way at a gig.

> *I love the Gary V adage of always viewing any deal or interaction with another person as you giving 51% and taking 49%.*

This isn't about you being subservient, it's about making sure the other person feels valued. If you're on a gig and the venue bring you sandwiches when it said on the contract that you'd get a hot meal, don't make a massive fuss. It's not that hard for a grown-arse adult to get themselves some food. And it's hugely important not to be a dick with fans. How much time you spend interacting with them and how you treat them on a gig makes such a difference.

Any time I do a gig I want to be the last one out the door because then I know I've worked the room as much as I can. I say thank you to people who are leaving, I take photos with them, I stop to talk to them, anything I can do to show I appreciate them. I'm exactly the same with any other bands who are playing, the staff at the venue and the sound guys. I want to make sure that I leave with everyone saying, 'That was nice and easy, what a great bunch of guys, we'll have them back again.' At the end of the day, that sound guy might be looking for a band for a festival or that venue could be looking for a monthly slot or a band for a preferred recommendations list. You never know what or who is around the next corner so why make it harder for yourself? Life's so much easier when you're not a dick because everyone is so much nicer to you!

It's going to be OK

BIMM was eight or nine years old and we'd taken it from starting in my living room through to a university in two cities, about to go to a third, and we'd gone from 180 students to 2,000. But in spite of – or perhaps because of – this success, things were getting strained and stressful and I was not enjoying working there anymore, and I'm sure my colleagues probably weren't enjoying working with me either! The original plan for BIMM was that we would always keep our numbers limited, so we could deliver a level of care and attention for our students unrivalled by any other music college. I felt really disillusioned that we'd come so far from our original vision. Things finally reached breaking point at a meeting of the four directors, when the others told me that it clearly wasn't working. I instantly said that it wasn't a problem and I'd leave. I was 30 years old and assumed that it would be easy for me to go off and do something different. What actually ensued was a nine month, very messy business divorce. It was hugely stressful trying to sell my share of the company and in doing so, I lost a lot of friends. BIMM wasn't just something I built, it felt like a part of me. Pretty much every aspect of my life was tied into it but when I walked out of that door all of that stayed and I went home to sit in a room and watch TV.

Over that nine month period I lost a lot of confidence. The main aim of the other side's lawyers in a business divorce is to try and discredit everything you've done. I started to think negatively about myself and my abilities. I started to think that, as the youngest director by ten years, I'd lucked out and been taken along for the ride. I wondered if I was actually able to do anything on my own and worried that I was unemployable. I felt completely lost during that time and it was only over the next two years, as I began building my own business, that I started to get my confidence back.

Fast forward to a year ago when I bought a company for £1 million. In the final days running up to the sale the directors of the company, who are friends of mine, asked me what they should do once they'd sold the business and had a totally clean slate. They had no real idea of what was going to happen next. It was pretty much ten years to the day that I'd walked out of BIMM and it was great to be able to give them the advice that I wish someone had given me; that it was all going to be OK because the knowledge and experience you acquire when you build something counts for something and will stand you in great stead in the future.

It's exactly the same for musicians.

> *Every time you play a gig and write a song and make promotional content for social media it's another brick laid in the foundations of your career.*

Even if it all goes wrong, that experience will definitely count for something. Fear and insecurity might hit hard at first when you have to restart something but you'll be able to achieve in one year what took ten years before because of the knowledge and experience you've gained. See everything you do as valuable experience. Experimenting and learning is never wasted, one day you will need to call upon it.

Taking constructive criticism

Whenever I give musicians advice, whether it's via my online platforms, management business or educational initiatives, there's a bit of a running theme, which is that if I give them the advice they want to hear, I'm a hero but if I give them advice they don't want to hear, I'm an idiot. The biggest thing that holds musicians back is their inability to conform in the right areas. Musicians tend to be rebellious by nature. Once they leave school they don't want to toe the line and get a 'proper job', they want to play music and go on tour and stick two fingers up at the man and the system. The problem is, all too often rebelling against the system results in rebelling against yourself, and you end up sabotaging your career.

Musicians will spend hours and hours learning how to be the best they can be, getting lessons and advice and watching tutorials, but when it comes to carving a career path, they often want to make it up as they go along, making the same mistakes time and again. They don't like being told what to do, even if it means failing. The best way to improve and succeed is to seek out people with experience and ask them for advice and guidance and constructive criticism, then see how you can implement their advice in what you're doing.

When I was a kid I used to play an Ibanez bass. I loved it but it was a piece of shit, not a professional bass by any standard. I loved it because it was mine, for purely nostalgic reasons. When I was at music college my mentor, Bruce Dickinson, used to frequently take the piss out of my bass and bang on about why I needed a 'real guitar'. I told him all the plus points the shop had told me, which incidentally had nothing to do with whether it was a good guitar. One day Bruce sat me down and said, 'We joke about your guitar all the time, but I have made records and had a number one album and I can promise you that is not a good enough instrument for you to build a career on.' He was absolutely right, I'd just been too pig-headed and stubborn to take it in. I was only 18, with one failed album, I knew nothing compared to him. I'm so glad I finally took his advice. I probably wouldn't have had a career as a bass player if I hadn't. Don't get me wrong, I think it's great to experiment and be creative and original but –

> *learning to take constructive criticism from musicians with way more experience than you can be invaluable and one of the fastest tracks to success.*

One final note of caution when it comes to constructive criticism, it can be really easy to seek out the advice of friends and family but don't forget that they're not going to want to hurt you, so their feedback might not always be entirely honest. It's always best to seek out people with no skin in the game so to speak, the people who aren't trying to protect you and are trying to help you.

Dealing with haters

There's a massive difference between criticism that's designed to help you progress and grow and feedback that's purely negative and hurtful. Sadly, it's highly unlikely that you won't encounter some kind of hate in your music career. We've never lived in a time where it's been so easy for people to give direct feedback to musicians. Nowadays, music is free for everyone to comment on. Ditto you personally if you're on social media. Jealousy plays a massive part in the mindless hate you can get online and the more successful you become, the more the haters will have to be jealous of. I know it can be really hard to take but know that if you are getting a certain amount of negativity you must be doing something right because it means your message and music are getting out there. You're saying and doing enough for certain people to disagree and not like it. This is not always a bad thing. If the feedback you're getting is rosy all the time it's probably because you only have your friends and family following you!

Everyone will remember the first few times the hate happens because it's so unexpected and out of the blue. So often, the keyboard warriors say things in comments they'd never dare say to your face and this can be very hard to turn a blind eye to. You start to question yourself and what you did to deserve it. You can try and laugh it off but it takes someone pretty psychotic to not be affected by personal hate.

Recently, I posted a video on my YouTube channel, which unleashed a tsunami of comments. A lot of them were positive but there was also a shed-load of hate – including my very first death threat! Funnily enough, the video was called Stop Selling Music, which was a bit of a click-baity title, but I genuinely intended it to be a helpful video (just as I intend the same for this book), asking musicians if they'd be better off trying to monetise another aspect of their brand. I received 500 comments in first 24 hours. Then I made another video, offering musicians other ideas for sources of income and things went crazy on my YouTube. I was probably getting a new comment every three to five minutes and they were coming thick and fast on my Instagram and Facebook too.

Then something really strange happened. I started scanning the comments and if I saw positive words I'd skim over the message, perversely seeking out the ones with 'twat' or 'fucking idiot'. Even worse, I'd then start trying to have a debate with the haters. I feel like I'm an incredibly strong person mentally but by ten o'clock that night I was sitting on the sofa with my girlfriend Ella, still scanning the comments for hate, despite feeling really drained. Then I got a death threat in the comments, telling me I was a disgrace and they were going to come and chop off my head. They even sent me a link to a video showing someone being beheaded!

The thing to remember is that people deliberately go too far on social media to try and get a rise out of you. So you have to be ready for it, just like a fighter has to prepare themselves for being punched. No matter how good they are, at some point they're going to get hit. It's so important to keep it in perspective. One positive from my recent experience is that I got 5,000 new subscribers in two weeks. Weirdly the negative comments have helped as well as cursed me. It's a double-edged sword.

My advice to you would be to not engage at all with the haters. After all, you wouldn't engage with a ranting psycho on the street. If they're not being rational you're not going to solve anything by getting sucked into a conversation with them. There's nothing wrong with making someone look silly by presenting your side of the story, but do it calmly and good-naturedly. Remember, most haters do what they do to try and feel better about themselves, it's really nothing to do with you and the quality of your music. In conclusion:

haters gonna hate, but creators gonna create.

Part Ten: Self-Management

Most people tend to fall into one of two categories; they're either creative or they're logical and organised. Therefore, it can be quite difficult for musicians, who are creative by nature, to jump into the organisational management side of things. Whilst creatives obviously need to be able to create, in this day and age it's hard to achieve success as an artist without targets and goals and thinking about things in an organised and structured way. So, how can a musician organise and manage themselves to success? All of the staff in my office apart from my PA are musicians. So I know for sure that musicians can be organised and they have got it in them to manage things. The trick is learning how to do it and making it a priority. This part of the book is all about stopping making excuses and taking control of your career.

What do you want?

Setting clear targets and goals is the easiest way to focus your energy and achieve success. If you've set yourself a target, every time you do something you can ask, *is this helping me achieve my goal?* I would say that 80-90% of the musicians I meet know what they're doing but they don't have a clear objective in sight. Creatives tend to get very excited by any opportunities that arise and say, 'ooh yeah, I could do that.' Then all of a sudden, you've got yet another finger in yet another pie. Musicians need their fingers for playing, not for pies. Spreading yourself too thinly dilutes your time and energy and removes the focus from what you're really trying to achieve. I spend a lot of time trying to get musicians to answer the question: *What are you ultimately trying to do?* If you can't answer that question right now you need to focus on it more than anything else in this book. Sometimes musicians will answer the question, telling me, 'I really want to make a living as a musician...' then they add the little word 'and', and stick another answer on to the end, like... 'tour the world as a session musician'.

You need to have a clear and focused end goal. I'm not talking about a five year plan, that's something an accountant would have. Get away from that kind of thinking and focus instead on your purpose. What do you want your legacy to be? What do you want to look back on at the end of your life? A five year legacy just doesn't have the right ring to it.

I can sum up what I want my legacy to be in just 13 words: *I want to be the number one music industry educator in the world.* I want to be the guy that every musician thinks of when they want to learn something about the industry. That's my goal.

You have to believe in your target. If you say it but don't believe it, you'll keep getting detoured into other areas and sticking your fingers in other pies.

If you believe in your target, you won't take a detour.

At least three times a week, if not more, I'll start the day by writing down my end goal i.e. to be the number one music educator in the world. I do this to remind myself of what I'm working towards, so when I'm offered stuff that would be a detour, I'll remember that it doesn't fit into my target. I like to keep my goals as simple and minimal as possible. I don't want a page of things to achieve or a vision board crammed with loads of different things. I stay focused on my end goal – the biggest of the big – the thing I'm ultimately working towards. As I said before, we're living in a world full of distractions, so we need focus.

Can you sum up your long-term goal in one sentence? You might have lots of different targets and ambitions but once you have that one overall goal you can measure everything else you do against it. For example, if your overall goal is to be a hit songwriter, is playing guitar in your mate's band as a session musician helping or hindering that ambition? It's so easy to get overwhelmed by all of the opportunities available. Getting clear on your overall goal helps relieve the pressure and gets you focused.

Motorway analogy

Something I talked about in my last book, *The Rule-Breaker's Guide to Social Media*, is the motorway analogy. This is where a musician will tell me what they want but when I ask them what they're currently doing, it doesn't line up with their goal. It's a bit like someone asking me how to get to Manchester from Brighton, but when I tell them they need to take the M6 motorway as it leads straight to Manchester, they tell me they'd rather take the M4, even though it goes straight to Wales. When you're deciding on your targets and goals you have to stay on the right route and not take junctions off it. Unless you make something happen it won't happen because you didn't commit to it. You can't afford to be passive or wait and see what happens.

Once you've got clear on where you want to go, look at the road you're already on. What are you doing as a musician right now? Is it taking you on the right route? If you really want to be a metal musician and you're studying a jazz degree it's safe to say you've gone on a major detour. Or if you want to be a session player but you're spending most of your time song-writing, you've probably been diverted too.

It comes down to sacrifice again. Staying on the right route will inevitably mean going without certain opportunities, relationships and experiences. Musicians going on cruise ships is a great example of this. It's good money, great fun and an amazing life experience, but it won't help you achieve any other musical goals. If you want to be in a signed band you're not even on dry land, let alone the right motorway. Yes, you can take a detour but it's all about momentum. If you go and do a cruise for three or six months you've lost that time to other people competing for the same end goal as you. Don't forget that this is a very hard industry to succeed in. You need to be focused.

The art of focus

We're living in a time where distraction has become an integral part of living. Technology might be making our lives easier but it's making it a lot harder too. As well as constantly pinging with notifications, our phones let us watch videos, play games, check our social media, find a new partner, order a pizza... The list is endless. Everything is instant and there for the taking and it's too much. Coupled with that the fact that we're now expected to be all things to all people i.e. the artist, agent and sales and marketing manager, there's never been a worse time to be so easily distracted.

Usually, when you sit down to work for two hours you'll be lucky to get thirty minutes of concentrated time because of your phone pinging, ads popping up and people needing to get hold of you. Our brains are being pulled in ten different directions at any one time. No matter who you are or how smart, if you try and focus on several things at the same time it will not work. We need to find a way to get organised and focused in order to achieve the targets we're setting.

Let me ask you right now, how have you been distracted while you've been reading this book? Has your phone lit up with a notification or call? Have you broken off to scroll through Twitter, or taken a dip into Instagram? What have been the distractions for you?

Now I'd like to present you with a challenge: I'd like you to go into your phone and turn off every single notification for the next few hours while you do some work. At the end of the allocated time check how many notifications you've missed. I can guarantee that none of them will have been an emergency. No-one would send you a tweet to tell you that your house is on fire, using the flame emoji. The world won't have ended because you turned your notifications off for a few hours, but you will have got a lot more work done.

Once you've counted up the number of notifications you missed, work out how many there were per hour. It can be a sobering exercise when you realise how many things are trying to take your mind off the thing you're trying to do. On a more positive note, how much more work did you get done? How did it feel being able to focus so fully and gain some proper momentum?

Time-management vs priority management

I hear the excuse, 'I have a time management problem' about thirty times a week. Over and over again, people tell me they don't have enough time and they have too much to do. I'd like to challenge that. The truth is:

> *few of us have a time management problem but many of us have a priority management problem.*

If you're saying you don't have enough time for your music career but you've got enough time to watch eight hours of Netflix, go out with your mates and finish *Red Dead 2*, then I'd suggest it's your priorities not your time that needs managing.

We all have twenty-four hours a day, seven days a week. If you sleep for eight hours a day it still leaves you with sixteen hours. If you work for eight hours a day and have four hours for friends and family, you still have four hours free. That's a lot of time, in which you can get a lot done. But this time usually get sucked away by distractions. If most people who say they have a time management problem took an honest inventory of their diary for the week and logged how much time was spent on games, TV, social media browsing etc, they'd soon realise how much time was being wasted.

This is where it helps to go back to your ultimate goal and ask if everything you're doing is working towards it. Ask yourself what you can sacrifice to give you more time, what are the priorities you can lose. I think everyone can find an extra couple of hours a day if they need to. You have to be brutal about your priorities, which admittedly can be horrible, especially if you're having to choose between time with your loved ones or working on your band. But it all comes back to how badly you want it. It's the people who are able to lose certain priorities who make the biggest difference to their career because it buys them time and focuses them on where they want to go.

Try seeing your day in terms of percentage points. Every day has 100 points and it's impossible to add any extra. How will you allocate your points today? How many points will you dedicate to your family and social life and making money? And how many points will you dedicate to your music?

Time-keeping tips

Full disclosure: I'm not very organised with my time. I'm really good at priority management but not at all at time management. I don't like to be late but I don't get as much done as I'd like because I'm not very disciplined and tend to get over-excited and run over with things. I'm lucky enough to have a PA and her number one job is to manage my time. This is very different to managing a diary, which is simply a matter of plonking things in. Managing time is all about seeing how time can be squeezed to get the most from it. If I'm left to my own devices when it comes to time I'll sit having a coffee for an hour with someone after a meeting. My PA's job is to trim away all of the time wasted and schedule meetings and appointments for exactly as long as they need to be.

It's fascinating how much more you can get done when you view time like this. For example, if you tell me I've got two hours to write a blog post, it will take me two hours to write a blog post. But if you tell me I've only got one hour, I'll still get it done. It's just that in two hours I'll procrastinate more and take it slower.

Now, I can imagine most people reading this thinking, or maybe even shouting, 'I haven't got a PA or the money for one, stop showing off, you twat!' which I totally understand. But you can still find someone to help manage your time for free. Ask a friend, colleague or family member if you could chat to them about your goals for the week and if they could help you allocate your time accordingly. That way, you can create a proper structured schedule and even set your phone with reminders for what you're supposed to be doing and where you're supposed to be. Have some kind of accountability when it comes to your time-keeping.

For me, time is the most valuable thing in the world, so I want to make sure I'm not wasting or abusing it. One of the last things I do in the evening is write a list of the things I want to achieve the following day. Other things might come up on the day but at least I'm clear on what I want to achieve and I'm setting my day up for success instead of wondering what I'm going to do.

Learning songs

As a musician, learning songs should become second nature – a part and parcel of the job – but you wouldn't believe how many musicians learn songs in an inadequate way. When it comes to wanting a career, whether as a session player, a working musician or a teacher, the notion that you just need to have a rough idea for a song will hamper you hugely. Not only does it show a massive lack of respect for the song but it also indicates laziness and a lack of attention to detail. Bruce and I used to have a motto that we lived by:

you don't learn songs until you can play them,
you learn them until you can't play them wrong.

Genius is in the attention to detail. You need to learn songs to the highest standard. The person auditioning you will be auditioning others. They will know if you haven't learned it properly and put the time in. Think of the impression that gives. The good news is, the more songs you learn, the faster you get at learning, which is great because if you want a long term career, you need to learn songs quickly and incredibly accurately.

Here are some tips to guide you when it comes to learning...

- Can you perform the track without the vocals? This is very important as it will happen in certain auditions.
- Do you know the track well enough in order to transpose it on the spot?
- Do you know the styles needed to make the track sound authentic? For example, if you're playing a funk track how is your funk tone?

If I was going to an audition for a band and they gave me three songs to learn I'd probably learn ten. In doing so, not only am I going above and beyond but I'm getting into the mindset, technique and playing of that band.

When my brother-in-law was 18 he had an audition for a Queen tribute band – a national touring band who played to a thousand people a night. The band had an obvious set of ten of Queen's biggest hits. My brother-in-law was the youngest person at the audition by a country mile. To try and compensate for this he didn't just learn the songs they played live, he learned countless album tracks too, so that he could immerse himself in John Deacon's bass lines. When he turned up at that audition he was more like John Deacon than any other bass player there and he got the gig. If they had decided he was too young, he wouldn't have been to blame as he'd done everything in his power to get it. It's a great example of how putting the extra effort into learning songs can pay off hugely.

Conclusion

The most important lesson I want you to take from this book is that we are living in a time where you are in control. For the first time in the history of the music industry the power falls directly to the creator and the artist. The gate-keepers have been relieved of duty and the barrier to entry now resides in your creativity, talent, work ethic and belief. Whether you want to make a living or tour the world with your music, this IS the best time to make it happen.

Whenever you get stuck or feel overwhelmed, take a deep breath and think about your ultimate goal and one simple thing you can do to work towards it. At the end of the day, building a career is about 10,000 steps and not one giant leap.

Never stop learning and never stop experimenting. What worked yesterday might not work today and what worked for someone else might not work for you. There are good people out there who can help and give you the advice and support you need. I hope it's clear that I am one of those people and I want you to succeed as much as you do. Find the people who don't feed you bullshit and who will call you out when you need a kick up the ass. Those are the real heroes!

Lastly, always remember that the life of a musician is a privileged one. The ability to make memories, friends, money and life changing opportunities from your talent and music is amazing. Enjoy every rehearsal, gig, tour, studio day and appreciate that what you have is a life of privilege, albeit one that you work hard for. Look after your passion and it will return the favour.

Now let's go make shit happen! Turn the page for my 30 Day Challenge...

30 Day Challenge

I t's all very well reading a book on how to maximise your chances of success in the music industry but nothing beats putting the tips and advice you've read about into practice. In this final section of the book, I want to push you out of your comfort zone and get you organised, focused, and crystal clear on your targets. If you put in the effort and do each of the following challenges, I promise it will help you over the coming months and years of your journey.

Day 1: Main goal challenge

One of the biggest challenges facing musicians is staying focused on their main goal because there can be so many other distractions. In order to achieve success you need a clear destination and a coherent strategy in how to get there. Today's challenge is to think about your end goal. What is it that you want to achieve for your Plan A? Is it money? Fame? Acclaim and recognition? Security? Next, start thinking about your end goal in terms of your music. Do you want to take over the world with your originals band? Or do you want to be more of a hired gun as a session player? Or is your end goal simply to make enough money from music to be able to leave your day job?

I find it really funny when musicians say that their Plan A is to take over world with their band but failing that, they'll 'just' become a session player. This is like someone saying, 'I want to be a world class footballer but failing that, I'll just become a Formula One racing driver.' Both are equally hard to achieve so you can't look on one as an easier fall back option. You need to respect how hard all of these things are. Don't fall for the illusion that you can do well in many different areas. The reality is, if you want to do really well in your covers band, it will be a full time job in itself. Ditto originals bands. Don't disrespect the magnitude of what you're trying to achieve by putting time and effort into other things, like helping a mate out with their band. This will only water down the chances of your success.

CHALLENGE: Write your end goal in one concise sentence... of no more than 5 words!

Once you've got your end goal written down this concisely, you can use it as a benchmark against everything you do, asking if what you're doing is helping you achieve that five word goal. If it's not, then you're slowing yourself down.

Day 2: Setting yourself up to succeed challenge

Before we get stuck into all of the opportunities open to you it's really important to set yourself up to succeed. This challenge is all about acknowledging how much time you've got, what your best skills are, who you can call upon for help and collating your resources. It's about getting organised so you can build momentum.

CHALLENGE: *Write down your answers to the following questions:*
- How much time have you got to dedicate to your music and when?
- What are your best skills – in life and as a musician?
- Who can you call upon to help – friends, family, other musicians?

Now, break down your main goal from yesterday's challenge into realistic targets for the coming year, month and week, making sure that these smaller goals fit your resources. For example, if your main goal is to sell a million records but everyone in your band works in day jobs for 40 hours a week and has kids and you can only rehearse for three hours on a Wednesday, is this goal realistic? If not, readjust your goals accordingly. It's crucial that your resources match what you want to achieve. You need to be constantly working at it in baby steps.

Day 3: What's your story challenge?

This is one of my favourite challenges and it doesn't matter whether you're in a covers or originals band or you're a music teacher, all of you will need to grow a brand around your story. Storytelling is the fastest way to grow a brand and your backstory needs to be apparent to any new follower you get online. People need to understand who you are and what you stand for and what your story is so that they can come with you on your journey. Think about a long-running TV series, like *Friends* or *The Office*. It doesn't matter how late in the day you start watching the series, you'll easily pick up the characters' stories because they're constantly being recapped. But so many bands don't do that. They don't tell us where they've come from or how they've got there. We're expected to jump straight in at whatever point they're currently at. I'm not saying that you should keep repeating the same old backstory post. The great thing about social media is that the platforms offer places where you can keep your backstory visible, such as a pinned post on Twitter, Instagram highlights or the Facebook About section.

CHALLENGE: *Find a way to tell the story of where you've come from, who you are and where you're going, so that anyone can catch up with the story easily.*

Your story can be told in many different ways. The entire story could be told in one picture if you're clever. For example, if you're a wedding covers band, use a photo of you performing where the crowd – and bride – are clearly having an amazing night. Your story doesn't necessarily have to be told with words, just as long as it's told in a way that anyone can see it at any time on each of your platforms.

Day 4: Practice schedule challenge

It doesn't matter how experienced you are as a musician, you can always become better.

CHALLENGE: Come up with a practice routine designed to help you improve individually as a musician. Use the following three steps to guide you...

- **Step One: Time**
  I'll leave it up to you to decide how long you've got to devote to your practice every day. But I would say that it's more important to practise for shorter periods more consistently than for huge chunks of time with big gaps in between. Routine is key. Make sure you add in some research time too, for taking in and learning new ideas.
- **Step Two: Goals**
  Get clear on what your goals are for your practice. What are you trying to improve – and by when?
- **Step Three: Categories**
  Break your practice down into categories. For example, exercises, scales, ear training, theory, sight reading, improvisation and song-writing. You need to choose which is important for you and what you want to prioritise. I probably wouldn't practise everything every time. Think of it like a gym session. If you go to the gym three times a week you will focus on different areas of the body each time. Pick two or three things to specialise in per practice session.

Day 5: Recording yourself challenge

Recording yourself while playing in order to watch it back and critique your performance is one of the fastest ways to improve as a musician. And as I said earlier in this book, there's no excuse not to record yourself because nowadays everyone has a recording device in their pocket in the form of their phone.

CHALLENGE: Set up your phone to film yourself playing a track so you can study your entire technique.

Once you've made your recording watch it back and write down three things you could do to make it better next time. Then work on those three things for half an hour and film yourself again. If you feel comfortable with your performance this time, why not post it on your social media?

Day 6: Mentor challenge

Today I want you to start trying to find a mentor for your music.

CHALLENGE: Go through your contacts on your social media, phone, email and friends and acquaintances and draw up a list of people you'd love to learn something from.

Once you've drawn up your list I want you to message them one at a time and tell them you want to improve as a musician and you're looking for a mentor to help hold you accountable and achieve your goals. It's important to be respectful in your approach. Be prepared for them to say no and if they do, still say thank you. You never know, something might come of it later. Be respectful of their time too – make it clear that you don't need a lot from them, just a few tips and ideas now and again over email or a cup of tea – don't ask for the world. And have a think about what you could do for them in return. Whether it's some kind of financial reimbursement or helping them in some other way, such as sharing their content. We're living in a really good trade economy. Another way to win a potential mentor over could be to show them how talented you are so that they'll want to be a part of your success.

Day 7: The metronome challenge

For this challenge it doesn't matter what instrument you play or if you're a vocalist. I want you to practise using a metronome.

CHALLENGE: Perform a track of your choice, preferably something semi complicated, at 120 beats per minute.

Everyone thinks that it gets harder when you speed the tempo up, and to a certain extent it does, but today we're going to slow things down. So now I want you play exactly the same groove at 60 beats per minute. And then, if you think that's easy, take it down to 40 bpm – still playing the same thing. And for expert level, try a shuffle groove at 40 bpm, again any instrument can do this.

We can all play in time but there's different levels of playing in time. Hopefully this challenge will show how you can always be working on your timing to improve it. Figure out what tempo feels good to you, then slow it down incrementally. And when that speed starts feeling good, slow it down again. You can also do the same exercise increasing the speed. When you're able to play well extremely fast or slow it feels amazing when you play at the normal speed.

Day 8: Rehearsal plan challenge

Today's challenge is to organise your next few rehearsals. First and foremost, you need to get clear on the reason for you to rehearse. Is it for a show? Or to get the band tight? Or is it more of a creative session for song-writing?

CHALLENGE: Use the following tips to help you plan your next rehearsal...

- Write a list of the aims and objectives for the rehearsal.
- Plan how you can record the whole rehearsal.
- Decide whether you need a metronome – I would definitely recommend.
- Communicate with your bandmates beforehand about the penalties for lateness, taking too long to set up, or not having done your homework. In one of my bands we used to have a really embarrassing hat that people had to wear if they messed up. Or it could be that anyone who messes up has to get the beers in when you go to the pub after. Penalties can be fun but there's a serious side too, it's all about encouraging respect and getting people to see that there's a consequence to their actions.
- Allocate a musical director to oversee your rehearsal. That person needs to make sure you achieve the rehearsal objectives, like the chair of the meeting. They need to make sure you get to where you want to be.

Day 9: Rehearsal day challenge

It's rehearsal day and you can either see this as a chill out time with your mates, knocking through some tunes, or you can see it as a huge opportunity to get things done. The more you appreciate how much opportunity there is in the rehearsal room, the more it will drive you to work fast and efficiently, to get the most out of the few hours available to you.

CHALLENGE: Squeeze the lemon of your rehearsal using the following prompts...

- Go into your rehearsal focused on what you want to achieve, with a written list of objectives.
- Ensure your musical director chairs the rehearsal and allocates enough time to complete the objectives.

- Find ways of recording the rehearsal, whether audio or visual, and ideally take some notes of what was achieved so you can plan for the next one.
- Don't forget to use the opportunity of you all being together to do something creative for your socials.
- Lastly, make sure you are finding ways to improve the next batch of rehearsals and make them more productive. The best thing you can do is to make sure everyone is working hard and none of the band are turning up late, unprepared or slowing down the process.

The process of making and improving your music is fun and I don't want to sound like Monica from *Friends* when she says that 'rules control the fun', but rehearsals are an opportunity for you to really get some shit done. If you want to improve and build as fast as you can then this is the place to get started!

Day 10: Set list challenge

Full disclosure: I actually do this challenge sometimes for no reason other than I'm a geek! I like to print off a set list then cut it up into separate songs and spread them all over the floor so that I can arrange them into the perfect order. It helps to have a laptop handy for this one, so you can play the songs to hear their intros and endings and see how they fit together.

CHALLENGE: Print or write out your own set list, then cut it up into separate songs, lay them out on the floor and rearrange them into the perfect order.

Don't put songs in for the sake of it, see it as a coherent set, with everything needing to fit together perfectly. If you find that you don't have the right opener or the right song four, then write one. Also think about when you're going to have guitar changes.

I don't want you to do what you always do for this challenge. I want you to have an open mind. Look at your songs individually and ask where they fit perfectly into a set. If you discover that you've got four perfect songs for number six then you've got some work to do. This exercise can really help you up your game and give your audience something special.

Day 11: The gig booking challenge

Today's challenge is to find at least two gigs. Can you imagine if you did this every day? In one month you'd have 60 gigs booked, which would be a total game changer. I chose this challenge because I want musicians to realise that if they get really good at gigging because they're gigging a lot, the money will follow. The gigs you book at first might be an open mic night or a songwriters' night or a pub gig or a friend's party. It doesn't matter. The more you gig, the better you'll get and the more you'll increase your leverage and be able to charge more. I think musicians should get into the habit of collecting gigs like they do social media followers – it's a really solid route to success. 'Getting gigs from gigs' is a phrase we use every day in the office because gigging is such an effective way of getting more work in.

CHALLENGE: Set aside some time today hunt for gig opportunities. Try to get two booked in by the end of the day.

Day 12: Gig marketing challenge

Not being able to get enough people along to your gigs is an age old complaint from musicians. The fact is, in order to be a successful musician, you've got to be a great salesman too because you need to sell your brand and your identity.

CHALLENGE: Come up with a list of reasons for people to come to your gig instead of just expecting people to turn up.
Use these prompts to help you...
- Are you going to play new songs?
- Are you going to invite a special guest to come and play?
- Are you going to do some kind of competition giveaway?
- What value will you be giving to the people who come, other than just the privilege of seeing you play?

When it comes to marketing your gigs it's not just about awareness, it's about giving people a reason to want to come. Think about a gig you really wanted to go to in the past – it doesn't have to have been a massive band, it could have been a certain combination of bands. What made you really want to go and why?

Day 13: Show plan challenge

At the end of the day, the best way to get people to your gig is to be better than anyone else. If you're amazing live that will be the biggest draw. People will want to be a part of the excitement and energy. Therefore, thinking of it as a show rather than a gig is a crucial first step.

CHALLENGE: Write a list of all the ways you can improve your show, from the moment you walk on stage to the moment you walk off.
Can you improve the running order of your songs (see previous challenge)?

Can you improve your standing positions? Can the singer improve their fronting of the band? Will your audience know who you are? Are your clothes co-ordinated? And don't get me started on fungus beards! Today is your chance to iron out all these details. When it comes to your live show, genius is in the attention to detail.

When you've written your list of all the areas you could improve compile a list of ideas for *how* to improve them. Share this list with your band mates and ask for their input. Plan to record your next show so that you can see if all the things you've written down have been implemented well enough.

Day 14: Musicians' tool box challenge

When I was touring I went and bought a small hand-held tool box from my local DIY shop. It had loads of little box compartments and I filled them with everything I could think of to help out in a gig emergency. Things like spare strings, a spare strap, a screwdriver, a Swiss army penknife, a tuning winder, plasters, gaffer tape, blue tac, paper, pen, torch, metronome, nail clippers, string clippers and picks. And matches. *Top Tip: Matches are great if your guitar strap goes because you can stick two or three in the hole.* Grolsch bottle tops are great too. I'd always have a couple of them in my toolbox because the red washers work really well over the strap lock to stop it slipping off.

Effectively, creating this was my way of making myself as indispensable as possible to any band. Armed with my trusty toolbox it was like I became the dad of the band, someone to be relied upon in an emergency. I think that tool box probably got me 50 gigs as a dep bass player because I was always able to help musicians in their moment of panic and need, if they'd broken a string or forgotten a lead. The best thing was the box was only about a foot long, so it hardly took up any extra space.

CHALLENGE: Put your own gig-saving toolbox together.

Day 15: Gear challenge

Today's challenge is to carry out an MOT of all of your gear to find out what's working for you and what isn't. From my experience of working with and training thousands of musicians, gear is the number one thing that lets them down. In a nutshell, if you bring the wrong kind of gear to a gig or an audition it reflects badly on you.

Here are some common issues...
- Guitarists with a far too complicated pedal set-up.
- Bass players who don't have a loud enough bass amp.

- Singers with no mic.
- Musicians with leads which are crackly.

For today's challenge, I want you to think specifically about the five minute festival set up. Imagine that you've been given the opening slot at a festival in front of 10,000 people. It's a great opportunity to promote your band but because the festival organisers are doing you a favour, you're given just five minutes to get your stuff on before you perform three songs and then you're off. If you aren't set up and playing within those five minutes, it will eat into your 12 minute gig slot. So, what are you taking and what is your set up for those three songs? The number of musicians I've seen with this opportunity who try and take two or three guitars on stage plus a pedal board with 15 pedals and leads and drumsticks that look 20 years old, is shocking. All they're doing is setting themselves up to fail. Today's challenge is about setting yourself up to succeed. If you've got 15 pedals and leads you've got 15 chances for things to go wrong.

CHALLENGE: Get clear on how you can simplify your setting up process. Simplicity is key!

Day 16: Photoshoot challenge

To repeat what I said earlier in this book, photos are almost always the first impression people will get of you online. It's the thing their eyes will be drawn to on your social media or website and you need to make sure that they sum up who you are and make the viewer want to find out more. Just like profile pictures on Tinder, it's also important that your photos are up to date. Nobody wants the disappointment of an out of date you.

CHALLENGE: Set up a photo shoot.

While you can pay for a professional photographer, there are certainly ways you can save money by doing this yourself, as long as you know someone with a creative eye for photos. I definitely wouldn't recommend trying to do it by yourself using a timer. Take a look through your Instagram feed and find the friend with the most creative well shot pictures. Then message them and ask if they'd be willing to take some shots of you and your band as they're clearly so good at it. Chances are they'll be hugely flattered and will want to help. Once you've done that I want you to research three to five locations for a photo shoot – inside and outside, in case of bad weather. I really want you to put the time into finding a location that sums up your brand. This is where you can raise the bar over most other musicians/bands/artists, who out of laziness, will do a photo shoot in a rehearsal room. Be creative and think of the colours and the surroundings. Here are a few suggestions to help you...

- a quirky hotel
- a cool local bar
- a local children's play area
- a crazy golf course
- on a bus
- by a monument in your area

Make the setting fun for the viewer. Then think about what everyone's going to wear. Plan this in advance and make sure everyone's beard and hair are on point. Plan what props you want to take to the shoot – these could be your instruments or something completely random and wacky, like a typewriter or an old-style telephone.

Make sure you've got enough time at the shoot to set the scene beforehand. Don't just walk in and take the pic. Try different angles and poses and get plenty of different shots. Give the photo shoot time to bed in. You'll definitely take better pictures after an hour than just five minutes because you'll have relaxed a bit. And don't forget, all of this can be done on a phone if it's planned in advance and the lighting is good.

Once the photos are edited and back, go through all of your socials and add them to your feeds and stories and profile pics. And remember, photo shoots are a really powerful way of keeping people up to date with your journey, so don't leave it too long before the next one.

Day 17: Video challenge

If I was still a musician I'd probably use video to promote myself every day because it's so easy and cheap to play something, edit it and get it in front of people. And the more people are seeing you, the more you're staying in their minds. I'm shocked by how many musicians don't make videos of themselves, or if they do, it's once in a blue moon. I get hundreds of messages a day from musicians and often I'll click on their profile to see who they are and what they're doing. I'm always shocked by how few videos there are of them playing. Videos help you stand out from the crowd and bring value through your performing.

CHALLENGE: Record yourself playing for your personal social media, either a song or a riff or a groove.

Whenever I suggest this people talk about sound issues – especially if I'm talking to a drummer, guitarist or bass player – to which I say, yes, sound can be an issue, so find a way. Find the right location, a room that looks and sounds

114

good. And remember, you get to choose what you want to play. You're not giving away everything, just showing the world a snippet of who you are and what you can do.

Day 18: Networking challenge

As previously discussed, networking is a necessary evil. Some people are naturally gifted at making friends and some, like myself, are socially awkward. The key is finding your medium. I feel very awkward going to an event and starting conversations with people. But that's where social media comes in because certain platforms, such as Twitter and LinkedIn, allow you to join in conversations without being invited. Another method is to create content that will start a conversation and bring the networking to you. Come up with your own leverage. It could be a piece of music or starting a debate on a certain subject. If I wanted to network with live agents I could send a video show-reel of my bands to them, asking for their expert opinion on what could be improved. It sounds simple but you've just opened the door.

A word of caution; every day I get a bunch of people messaging me out of the blue asking me to listen to their track but without having built any rapport or leverage beforehand, which they could have easily done with a bit more conversation. For example, they could have commented on one of my videos and asked a question to start a chat. Then, if they messaged to say they'd really value my opinion on their track and would it be OK to send it, I'd say absolutely, because we'd already be mid-conversation. Who do you want to reach out to? What do you want from them and how can you start the conversation?

CHALLENGE: Start three proper conversations with people today who could influence your career.
Be prepared for rejection. If you want to talk to three, you might have to approach 100.

Day 19: Merch challenge

Merch is probably now the most important money-making source for any musician, outside of live gigging. As I stated earlier, music can't get any more free and it can only get easier to consume. You need to use your music to look after and build your audience and monetise elsewhere. To do that, you need to have a product that's sellable. The obvious kinds of merch are CDs, vinyl and wearables. But we're now in an era where the winners when it comes to merch are the people who are the most creative. So don't just think of the obvious stuff like a t-shirt. Build an audience with your music then sell them whatever you want – a course or a performance, a piece of art, or other content. In this way you can build a brand to attach to your music. It could be fashion, art, education, or other entertainment but unlike your music, it has to be restricted until your audience buy it.

CHALLENGE: *Think of a piece of merch you can monetise.*

Think of it in terms of a business model. If you want it to be t-shirts, fine. But don't be afraid to think outside of the box. How about something random, like candles or shoes? Keith Urban sells his own brand of guitars at his gigs. I saw a band a while ago and the singer, who was an artist, was selling his paintings as part of their merch. They were all individual prints and they were very good. The band Enter Shikari sell books containing their lyrics and essays and photos and artwork, something for their fans to treasure. What could you offer your audience that they would want to pay for?

Day 20: Social media challenge

This challenge is all about getting your social media in order. There can be so many things to do on your social media platforms that you end up overwhelmed and do nothing. So many bands end up doing social media 101 where, if they've got a gig, they'll post about it. The trouble is algorithms have ripped away our reach and the only way we can get it back is if we're bringing value regularly. So today's challenge is all about creating a social media strategy. Forget trying to make a strategy for all of your platforms, let's concentrate instead on a couple of things you can do at a very high level. This challenge is more about the content you make as opposed to the platforms you share it on.

First of all ask yourself, *what can we do today to bring our audience value?* If you answered that question every single day you can then decide how it gets wrapped up, either in audio, video or text, and post it. Don't over-think it. It could be as simple as just playing something. Lewis Capaldi is smashing social media at the moment because he's a bit of an unlikely pop star. He's got a very Scottish accent and he looks like a foot. No matter what time of day it is, he looks as if he's just woken up. But what's brilliant is that he's real and he's taking his audience on a journey with him. He just had a number one album and a tour and he's been performing regularly on TV shows, including the Brits. Every day he takes us with him via his posts. We see his hotel rooms in different parts of world, we're taken backstage at his radio interviews. Effectively we're like a friend he's invited along for the ride. As he regularly posts small snippets of his day and how he's feeling and where he is, we feel as if we're a part of it.

You might be thinking, well it's all right for him, he's got a number one album. But don't underestimate how interesting musicians' lives are to non-musicians. Yesterday, I received a message from a guy who told me that because he lives in Russia, it's very difficult to get gigs. He wanted to know how he could get people to take notice of him. The first thing I thought was, I want to see what Russia looks like and what he feels when he's struggling and trying to break out. I was really interested in him and he's not playing the Brits. So don't forget that where you live and your personal experiences could be really exciting to someone else, even if they're boring to you.

CHALLENGE: *Plan a piece of content for your social media that you can scale.*

This could be a vlog or a weekly performance or a show. You can't just keep posting push media. Come up with an idea that will really bring value to your audience. It could be blog, or a video series or a podcast. What could you plan that you can keep running on a regular basis, along the same theme? What type of series could you build so that you have a model for replicating, week in week out? If you're not sure to begin with it could be as simple as doing a little 3 song gig every Tuesday, or a band Q & A show. Something that people will come to expect each week.

Day 21: Zombie apocalypse challenge

OK, while we're unlikely to have an actual zombie apocalypse, we are likely to have another recession – a financial apocalypse   and being prepared for that now will 100% help when the time comes. I've worked through two recessions. The first was in 2001, when we set up BIMM and the second was in 2008 when I set up DK Management. So I like a good recession because I'm prepared and I know what to do. Basically, I'm the guy in the zombie apocalypse who has the weapons and the secret hideaway.

What tends to happen in a recession is that panic sets in and people make silly decisions, usually trying to make more money from less consumers. As a musician, you need to go where the work/money is. And to survive you need to be able to sacrifice more than anyone else. When a recession hits you need to be able to live off very little money and put your ego to one side and take on work you might never have wanted to do before. You need to work harder for less and you need to be thankful while you're doing it. This is why I win during a recession because I can lower myself and tense that muscle for longer than everyone else. When the next recession hits, which it will because we go through one every ten or so years, I'll be ready because I've spent the last three years building up my personal brand. And that's what today's challenge is about, it's about recession-proofing yourself by building up a stock you can leverage.

CHALLENGE: Create a recession-proofing action plan.
First of all, write down all of your outgoings and all of your potential income sources. Not just what you're earning at the moment but if the chips were down, what else could you do to make money? And how could you trim your outgoings? In a recession it's not possible to make more money but view that time as a way of building collateral by providing value so that when the storm passes, you can cash in. People tend to become very selfish during a recession but if you embrace suffering and focus on really looking after people, it will pay back big time once the crash is over. What would you do if a recession hit tomorrow? Where would the money come from? How little could you live off? How could you give extra value in a time when people are holding on to their money and how long could you survive doing that?

Day 22: Irreplaceable challenge

In order to make yourself irreplaceable as a musician you need to figure out what you can provide on top of your skill. And more importantly, how you can commit to improving other things to make yourself more irreplaceable. For me, being irreplaceable is about responsibility. The more responsibility you take on, the more irreplaceable you become. Whether that's through playing second instruments or doing backing vocals, or whether it's driving or owning a PA, or taking on the responsibility of doing your band's social media, photography, videos or tour management. There are many different ways you can make yourself indispensable.

CHALLENGE: Have an irreplaceable brainstorm.
Create a list of all the extras you can provide and all the extras you could learn to do. What can you commit to doing for the next year, so that in one year's time you'll be more irreplaceable?

Day 23: The second instrument challenge

Most musicians tend to dabble in other instruments. Whilst I'm a bass player, I have done gigs playing other instruments or as the singer. When you've got bills to pay you have to find as many ways as possible to pay them. To learn a second instrument to a competent level just enough to gig could make a huge difference when the chips are down or in terms of getting a gig over another person.

CHALLENGE: Figure out how you can set yourself up with a second instrument.

This could mean allocating time to learning a new instrument from scratch or, if you can already play a second instrument, committing to a couple of re-hearsals and gigs to give yourself more confidence. If you are unsure of what to choose as your second instrument take a tip from me – you'll never struggle for work if you can play piano to a basic level. This is because there are so many more opportunities and a distinct lack of specialists in this area. You could play background music in a restaurant or teach piano lessons. People are always desperate for decent keyboard players and as an added bonus, it always helps your theory.

Day 24: Outside the box performing challenge

As a bass player, I always tried to think outside the box when it came to getting opportunities to perform. I approached yoga teachers about playing relaxing background music in their classes and I used to play bass in the background for a comedian while he told jokes.

CHALLENGE: Think of other places you could get gigs, and think outside the box.

Where could you offer to play to provide background atmosphere? If you're a vocalist, why not try an old people's home? You don't have to perform for a fee, you could just ask people to have a whip around. Are there any commu-nity-based businesses and organisations in your area that you could find your way into in order to make more money?

Day 25: Learning songs challenge

Learning songs is part and parcel of being a musician. My biggest bugbear is when covers bands want to get paid extra money for learning songs – that's what you're supposed to do! Learning songs should be an integral part of your practise, as a key way of being able to make more money. Knowing songs and being ready is the best way to kick-start a career because when a band need someone to step in at short notice and you're able to save the day, you very much have a way in. I used to contact all of my local bands and say, 'I'm a bass player, give me your set list and I'll learn it and if you ever need me to step in in an emergency, I'll be ready.' That got me about three gigs a week just from deps. You can make a really good living being a save the day mu-sician. Through our management company we have 1,500 gigs a year, which equates to anything up to 50 gigs a weekend. Should something go wrong with a car, a traffic jam, illness or injury, we've got to be able to cover that musician. It might be that we don't find out that a musician isn't able to make it until one hour before they're due to be at the venue. Other musicians who are willing to drop everything and dep at the last minute are invaluable to us and the first people we call on our replacement list.

CHALLENGE: Approach people with a view to learning their songs.

If you're a covers musician approach local agencies. Look at their top covers bands and find out their set list and start learning those songs – it's never wasted. If you're not into covers you can do the same thing with local originals bands and tell them that if they ever need a dep, you're available. Even if you don't get any work from this challenge it won't be wasted because you'll be training your ear to learn faster and you'll be raising your profile because you'll be messaging people and networking. I used to know a drummer called Smiley who would send a text message out every week saying, 'I hope you're all having an amazing day. I just wanted to let you know that I have an available slot this Saturday and if you need a smiley drummer give me a shout.' He was never short of work because he made it so easy for people to find him.

Day 26: Call to action challenge

Every piece of social media is a piece of online real estate and an opportunity to tell the world who you are and what you want them to do. Your job is to maximise every opportunity.

CHALLENGE: Create a clear call to action on your social media.

Think about what you want someone to do when they come into contact with any of your social media. It's important to get very clear on this. If you give your audience too many choices they can end up crippled by indecision. Do you want then to listen to your Spotify, sign up to your YouTube, or buy your latest merch? Rather than having five different messages, have a very simple message across everything. Use the following prompts to help you:

- Do you have a call to action on your email signature?
- Do you have a call to action on your Insta bio?
- Do you have a call to action in your Twitter About section?
- Do you have calls to action in your pinned posts on Twitter and Facebook?
- Do you have a slide show or video in your Facebook banner?
- Are there clear links to the place you want them to go?
- Are your profile pictures up to date and as professional as possible?
  Remember the importance of making a good first impression. No one will

heed a call to action if it looks crap. Take a good look at your banners, about section and bio and ask yourself if they're good enough and if not, what do you need to change?

Day 27: Social media batching challenge

Most bands can go missing in action online for ages, often because they haven't been together for a while. But if you plan your social media in advance you can stockpile content when you do get together. If you're at a rehearsal or gig and you know that you'll need six posts before you're next together, create that content in advance while you're there.

The key is to work a week in advance on your social media. That way you'll always have enough content and you'll never have the pressure of having to come up with something on the spot.

CHALLENGE: Plan your social media content for the coming week.
Figure out what kind of content you're going to create when your band get together and what sort of content could you make when you're not together. Approach it like a personal trainer batching nutritious meals for a week in advance on a Sunday evening. Sunday night could be your social media night, where you do your planning for the week. Get clear on what you need content wise and when you will be able to get it. Set an alarm on your phone right now – a reminder for every Sunday (or whichever day you choose for your planning and batching). Stick to this every single week and you'll soon be killing it on your social media.

Day 28: The image challenge

As I stated earlier in this book, whether we like it or not, we are working in a fashion-based industry. I know there are exceptions to this rule but on the whole, successful musicians will fit into a certain image. If you want to open the door to more opportunities don't fight against this – something I did for years – it's far better to embrace it and if need be, find someone to help you. Many musicians are geeks like me, thinking about music first and foremost, with how we look being a bit of an after-thought.

CHALLENGE: Enlist a third party's help with your image.
Rather than asking your partner or a family member to help, go through your Instagram followers and find someone who fits what you would class as a fashionable person. Or failing that, reach out to a local fashion student and ask for their advice. Give them a budget – it doesn't have to cost loads – and

guidelines regarding the type of music you're into and what you're comfortable wearing. Trust me, you will see massive results. I've always worn jeans and a t-shirt and I'm not fashion conscious in anyway. But a year ago I started a relationship with someone who's very into fashion and I took her advice regarding my image. The process was brutal – she threw out two thirds of my wardrobe! But in the time since I've got more work and I can't help thinking it's because I look way less like a student. Above all else, when you look better you feel better and way more confident.

Day 29: Thank you challenge

This one sums up quite a lot of the challenges we've had, in that it's all about looking to gain attention, add value, post more on your social media and find more work and opportunities. I think the phrase "thank you" is possibly the biggest door opener of all. Every time I get a thank you from someone about my work it makes me want start a conversation with them and find out how I can help them more. The same applies when creators I follow make a video saying thank you and show appreciation for me as an audience member – it makes me want to help and support them more.

CHALLENGE: Thank three people.

Today, reach out to three people you haven't seen for a while, whether it's been a month or five years, and simply say hi and tell them how much you appreciate them. I'm talking about reaching out to anyone here. Don't just go where the money is. You're not looking for anything in return for this challenge and I want you to try and do it as often as possible. The great thing about this challenge is, even though you aren't doing it to seek anything in return, I can guarantee that if you did it three times a day, in one month you'd have gained more work or opportunities from it.

Day 30: Review challenge

This one is all about going through the 30 day challenge and writing down what you have learned from it. What worked? What didn't? What could you have done better? What would you like to repeat and put into your daily schedule? How can you use the most effective parts of this 30 day challenge in order to move forward with your career?

A last favour

Thank you so much for buying, borrowing, or even stealing this book. The fact you have given me your time means so much and if it has brought you any value could I ask you to leave a review on Amazon? It sounds silly but every review means so much to me and not only do I read every one, but once in a while I sit and read through them and think about how lucky I am. And if you think I'm a knob-head then that's okay too! All that's left to say now is, if you need me you know where I will be. Please don't be a stranger. Now go and make something special that you can be proud of!

YouTube – Damiankeyes
Facebook – Damokeyes
Instagram – Damiankeyes1
Snapchat – Damiankeyes
Twitter – Damiankeyes
LinkedIn – Damiankeyes

Acknowledgements

I would love to take this opportunity to thank a few people, who make my life so much easier, who support my crazy hair-brained ideas and allow me to be creative, experiment and grow, both personally and in business.

To Siobhan Curham, my book writing partner. Thank you for taking my ideas and rants and turning them into a fully fledged book. Two down and we're just getting started! May there be a lot more pages written and biscuits eaten together!

To Bruce John Dickinson, who has been my mentor and partner since I was 19 years old. Bruce, you are the reason I believe so firmly in mentoring and education done well. You started my crazy journey and there is so much life left in us moving forward!

To my everyone at DK, Warble & Black Rock Media, thank you for this crazy adventure we are on and let's keep on striving to great things. Big Love!

To Tom Heron for designing yet another awesome book cover and for the great music with The Xcerts!

To my friends and family, what can I say except thanks for putting up with me.

And most importantly thank you to *you* for reading this, or for any video of mine you have watched, or for any comment, like, or even dislike, you have ever taken the time to leave. You inspire me to keep growing and looking for ideas and to stay creative.

Notes

Use the following blank pages to jot down your ideas for the 30 Day Challenge

Made in the USA
Middletown, DE
16 April 2020